The growth and
development of children

The growth and development of children

Third edition

Catherine Lee

Formerly Head of Department of Food, Health and Fashion
Oxford College of Further Education

Longman
London and New York

Longman Group UK Limited
Longman House, Burnt Mill, Harlow
Essex CM20 2JE, England
and Associated Companies throughout the world

Published in the United States of America
by Longman Inc., New York

First published 1969
Seventh impression 1976
Second edition 1977
Fifth impression 1982
Third edition 1984
Sixth impression 1989

British Library Cataloguing in Publication Data

Lee, Catherine
    The growth and development of children. — 3rd ed.
    1. Child development
    I. Title
    155.4   BF721

ISBN 0-582-29646-3

Library of Congress Cataloguing in Publication Data

Lee, C.M. (Catherine Macaulay)
    The growth and development of children.

    Bibliography: p.
    Includes index.
    1. Child psychology. I. Title.
    BF721.L443   1983   649'.1'019   83-5454
    ISBN 0-582-29646-3

Produced by Longman Group (FE) Ltd
Printed in Hong Kong

Contents

Introduction

There are a great many people working with young children in the field of education now who are not trained teachers — nursery nurses, playgroup leaders and helpers, assistants in nursery schools, classroom assistants and ancillary workers in infant and primary schools. Whatever their particular work is they influence the children and contribute to their education by virtue of being adults among them. However efficient they are at their work in the cloakroom or storeroom, playroom or classroom, in caring for material or serving meals, it is their attitude to the children and their behaviour towards them that count most.

If adults understand a little about why children behave as they do they will be able to respond to them more freely. We understand children's behaviour much better when we know something about their growth and development. This book does not set out to discuss methods of work so much as to try to look at how children behave as they develop from babyhood through the primary school years.

The examples of behaviour used throughout are from my records or from the observations of my students in nursery nursing and in courses for classroom assistants and playgroup helpers. I should like to record my deep affection and respect for these students with whom I have worked for thirty-five years, and my gratitude for the cooperation and friendship of the superintendents, matrons and teachers in nurseries, day-care centres, schools and playgroups in the Oxford area, and in Australia, the United States and Canada.

My friends in the Social Services Departments of Oxfordshire and Buckinghamshire have given me much help and advice for which I am most grateful.

I am greatly indebted to Mrs Jill Webberley, General Inspector with special responsibility for nursery and infant schools in Northamptonshire, who has cooperated with me in revising the last three chapters for this edition. She has had twenty-three years' experience in working with young children. Her administrative ability is combined with an outstanding perception of the needs of children and imaginative common sense in meeting them.

Chapter 1

Stages of development

Growth and development

We would not be working with children if we were not interested in them. We want to understand them and in order to do this we must know something about how they have become the personalities they are. Children are what their histories have made them and if we know a little about those histories we will understand to some extent why each child behaves as he does.

Although we talk a good deal about him there is no such person as the average child. Each child is a separate and unique person, different from all other children. Yet children, like adults, have much in common and all have developed in the same way, passing through the same sequence of stages in their development, although each has done so at his own pace and with his own equipment of body, temperament and abilities. It is important that we should know as much as we can about these stages of development for three good reasons.

The first is that if we know what to expect at each stage we are not worried, surprised or shocked at the children's behaviour. We know, for instance, that it is normal for a child to have no control of his bowels for the first twenty months of his life; we are not worried if a three-year-old bashes his teddy bear on the head and jumps up and down on it; we are not upset when a five-year-old boasts and shows off in an irritating manner or a six-year-old sulks and is contrary. We know that these forms of behaviour are quite usual and that the child will soon outgrow them. We also know that he may well revert to a type of behaviour which he has outgrown when he is under pressure — that is, when he is sick or tired or anxious or frightened — but that, again, this is a temporary thing and all the time he is growing away from his babylike behaviour. We can enjoy our children at each stage.

Secondly, if we recognise the stages of our children's development we can give them the things they need at each stage so that they can fully complete it before passing on to the next. We can make sure they get from us support and encouragement, or affectionate control, or help in solving problems, as well as all the material they need for nourishment of mind and body. We will not make the mistake of denying a stimulus without which they may not progress to the next stage nor the mistake of trying to teach them something they are not ready for. We shall not waste their precious time and energy at any stage by asking them to do something they are physically or emotionally or intellectually unable to do, such as sitting still or sharing playthings or writing.

Thirdly, we can spot danger signals and ask for skilled help. If we see a child behaving for too long in the manner of a stage he should have outgrown then we know that this immaturity is a sign that he needs help. If a child does not sit up by the time he is a year old, or is not walking by two, not talking by four, still having passionate temper tantrums at six, being fussy about his food at eight or not reading by nine, we know we must find help for him. These are obvious examples and there are many subtler instances of immaturity which we shall recognise with experience.

Bodily growth and skills

Children grow and develop from the moment they are conceived until they reach adulthood at about twenty years of age. Growth is continuous during that time: there are no periods when growth stops for a while and then begins again.

But growth does not always take place at the same rate; at some periods in his life the child grows faster than he does at other times. The first few months of his development in his mother's womb is the period of fastest growth — he never grows as fast again. The first year of his life after birth is the period of next most rapid growth. After that he grows a little more slowly until he is about four years old and then much more slowly until he reaches puberty, when he begins to grow fast again. After two or three years his growth rate slows down until he reaches his final physical size at about twenty.

To grow is to get bigger. To develop is to change in form as one grows. Children develop as they grow and every child passes through the same clearly recognised sequence of stages in development. His body changes its proportions and as his skeleton and his nervous system mature he gains more control over his movements. He sits up before he crawls, crawls or creeps or hitches before he stands, stands before he walks. He must reach a certain level of development in one stage before he can pass into the next stage.

Children do not all grow at the same rate, though they all follow the same general pattern. In the nursery we see some children of three who are as big as some of the four-year-olds and almost as skilful at climbing and running. Some children reach each stage of development earlier than others. For instance one baby will crawl at seven months while another will not reach the crawling stage till nine months. The baby next door is staggering about at ten months when our baby has not started to crawl. This does not depend on size. It is a matter of individual maturing. Girls tend to reach each stage of development earlier than boys.

Scientists and doctors who have been watching and measuring the growth of children have noticed that the process of developing has been speeding up during the last hundred years and children today are somewhat taller and heavier than children of the same age were a century ago. We can see this speeding-up over shorter periods, too. Textbooks written about forty years ago say that a baby usually doubles his birthweight by the time he is six months old. But babies today usually double their birthweight between four and five months. Children of five years now are as big as six-year-olds were forty years ago.

Intellectual and emotional development

Children do not only develop physically. They develop intellectually and emotionally too. It is more difficult to decide whether this development is like that of the body: continuous but faster at some periods than others. Most people who work with children believe that it is and believe also that intellectual and emotional development takes place by a sequence of stages. The only way that we ourselves can judge of this is by observing the behaviour of children we work with over a span of time.

Not only do children develop at different rates from each other, but the strands of physical, intellectual and emotional development in each child progress at different rates. So in any group of children of the same age we can see individual differences in development between the members of the group in every way. For instance we may have in a group of five-year-olds a boy not differing greatly from the others in bodily growth who is already able to read easily and to whom intellectual work appears to be easy but who is still not able to share his playthings and who still falls into tantrums like a two-year-old. At this stage we will not know whether he is a gifted child or is just ahead of the others in his intellectual development for the moment. The others may catch up with him in a year or two. He may in time catch up with them emotionally.

In the same group there may be a girl who, although smaller in body than the others, is learning to read and enjoy mathematics at about the same standard as the average for the group. At the same time she is emotionally mature. She forgets herself and calmly mothers the others, binding the group happily together by her influence.

There may also be a boy in the group much bigger and stronger than the others, steady, reliable and helpful but well below the average of the group intellectually.

Among the ten-year-olds one of the girls may already have entered puberty. She may be moody and restless, barely keeping up with the work of the group and losing interest. The other ten-year-old girls may still be some years away from puberty and content with their play and work, though they will vary in intellectual ability.

Although at any given time a child may seem to be lagging behind his age group in physical growth, or in intellectual development, we may find that he has caught up with the majority of his group a year or two later.

This does not mean, of course, that everyone will end up exactly the same as everyone else. We all begin life with different endowments, physical, intellectual and temperamental, and our life history — that is the way we affect our environment and it affects us — decides the way in which these endowments develop into the characteristics by which we become known. Some children will grow up to be taller or shorter adults than the majority of their age group, others will be cleverer, others will be better tempered or more optimistic or less reliable than their fellows.

As we work with children we are part of their environment, so we affect them and they affect us. The way a child behaves when he first goes to school may in part depend on the way he was weaned and his response to weaning. The way a group of children behaves to us when we work with them may affect the way in which we approach other groups of children. We can see the influence an interested home has on the education of a child, even one who goes to a poor school, and we see in the same way how an unresponsive home affects the progress of a child in the best of schools.

The developing child

Here is a brief account of the stages of development and the ages at which most children pass through them. Remember that each child is unique but that in a short work like this it is impossible not to fall into the mistake of generalising, thereby suggesting that children of any particular age all behave in the same way. Of course they don't! Correct my generalisations by watching the children you work with and try to see each one as a separate person.

The first year of life

The baby makes very great strides in the first year of his life. From being a completely dependent creature at birth he has become by his first birthday a restless, eager child about three times as heavy and eight inches longer, staggering about the room holding on to the furniture, almost able to feed himself, laughing at familiar friendly faces, distinguishing strangers, babbling happily most of the time, awake and energetic for ten or eleven hours out of the twenty-four. He has learned more in this year than he will ever learn again in the same period.

A great deal of research is being carried out at present on the abilities of newborn babies — how they see faces, remember them and react to them; how they hear sounds, locate them, react to them, remember them and recognise them; how they locate odours and turn towards or away from them; above all, how they act towards and interact with the adults who care for them, especially with their mothers. Most of this research is still in progress and has yet to be correlated but what does emerge so far is that the new baby is much more sophisticated in his response to his surroundings than was ever before realised, that he has a very great capacity for learning and that he is capable not only of responding to social approaches by his mother but of initiating them.

At birth The new baby is utterly dependent on the adults around him. He knows nothing of the world into which he has been thrust. He is conscious of changes in temperature, of being lifted and handled, of some sounds, of bright lights and of the closeness of another human body. But these are experiences he cannot control although he can react to some of them by slight movements. He cannot do anything for himself except breathe, suck and cry for help. He cannot move his body voluntarily except to turn his head sideways. He may wave his arms about and open and shut his hands but he does not choose to do this; his nervous system is not developed enough to give him control over his body. This control is gained in some measure over the next twelve months and the achieving of it is his main concern during the year. At birth his legs are small and weak and his head is disproportionately large.

Although he likes to be left undisturbed as much as possible and sleeps or dozes almost all the time, he can show quite clearly within a few hours that he is aware of fresh sensations and of human contact. Our African students tell us how content their babies are, carried by a fold of cloth on their mothers' backs close to their mothers' bodies. Most new babies fall asleep when cuddled close to their mother's body. But mothers also describe how their babies, only a day or two old, respond by alertness or slight bodily adjustments such as turning their heads or stiffening or by opening their eyes wide that they appreciate that something new is happening. That implies that they remember what has already happened to them. We realise now that a new baby can see more clearly when he is held upright than when he is lying down. A young mother who had just had her first baby wrote this:

> When Emily was a few days old she was with me in my hospital room. She began to cry and needed comfort. I picked her up and began to walk back and forth across the small room, holding her in a half-upright position. She stopped crying and gazed and gazed, apparently at the passing scene, and her eyes grew round and enormous.

His emotional life is crude. He cries vigorously when he is hungry, the cry turning to one of panic if he is left unattended for too long. His cry sounds outraged if he has stomachache and he may suck his hands if they are near his mouth. A mother writes of her two-day-old daughter: 'During the afternoon she was very much distressed by some pain and cried hard for a long time during which she sucked her hands with some appearance of desperation.' Some babies growl quite fiercely at physical discomforts such as hiccups or wind or bowel movements.

The baby is startled by loud, sudden noises. He jerks, throws out his arms and may cry. Being held loosely or dropped an inch or two into his cot brings the same response. He soon begins to show signs of contentment, though. Once he has been successfully introduced to the breast he sucks vigorously and seeks the breast by turning his head when he is in his mother's arms. The same mother reports, again on the baby's second day: 'She definitely shows excitement when she is hungry and put to the breast. She turns eagerly towards it.' When this baby was eight days old her mother wrote:

> This morning, at the end of the feed, after rejecting the nipple as usual, she played with it with her lips for some time and then suddenly seized it again and sucked vigorously for about a minute, finally rejecting it again. At almost every feed her

method is to suck strongly with only short, infrequent pauses for the first ten minutes and then to take longer and more frequent rests and to sigh, grunt and make noises of satisfaction during the next ten minutes.

These extracts from the mother's diary give a picture of the baby's first social contact. Of course the baby at this age has not any idea of his mother as a separate person since he has no idea of himself as a person either. She is only that part of his surroundings which brings satisfaction, warmth and comfort.

The needs of the baby during the first month are simple — warmth, sleep, as little disturbance as possible, firm, gentle handling, food, and a feeling of physical closeness with his mother.

One month   By the end of a month the baby has settled into a routine of life — feeding, sleeping and being bathed and dressed. He makes many small involuntary movements: spreading fingers; sucking thumb, fingers or whole hand; clasping one hand with the other; interlocking fingers; stretching up arms; clawing his face. With some babies this clawing movement seems to be indicative of pain or satisfaction. When in pain the baby claws desperately, when satisfied he claws gently and slowly. He fans his toes often, when stimulated by touch, or warmth of the fire, or even when there is no external stimulus. He makes movements of his head backwards or sideways and can lift his head briefly when his mother holds him to her shoulder. He seeks the breast with his mouth, often sucking the cheek or neck of his mother as she holds him when he is hungry. When awake, and sometimes when he is asleep, he constantly pouts, makes sucking sounds and grimaces. He grunts, sighs and makes squeaking noises during his sleep and often sighs as if with satisfaction when fed. His eyes now follow a hand moving in front of his face, and he stares drowsily at the ceiling or walls when he is awake. His mother's voice speaking or singing to him quietens him when he is restless but has little effect when he is very hungry. He will turn towards the sound of a clear voice close by when he is awake and content. He cries vigorously when he is hungry or wants attention. Some babies cry a good deal for the first two or three months and then, quite suddenly, they seem to enjoy life more and become contented and happy.

These first weeks of the baby's life are a critical time for him. It is true to say that they give him the foundation on which his future health depends. At this time he needs to feel loved and cared for in a very personal and intimate way by one person. Although, of course, he is not conscious that this is happening, he is at this stage making a deep and steady relationship with someone other than himself. If he is not given the opportunity to do this, that is if he is not cared for intimately and lovingly by one person, he may never become a fully responsive and responsible member of any society, able to make lasting relationships with other people, to love and to give freely. Fortunately most babies have their own mothers to care for them in this way, but for the staff of the residential nursery or the day nursery this period of the baby's life imposes special responsibilities. Fortunately, too, the practice of leaving the baby for long periods alone in pram or crib has gone. In most cases now the baby lies in his baby bouncer at an angle from which he can see well in the midst of the family from the beginning.

Three months   The baby at three months is alert, interested in life and delighted to be with other people. He smiles and uses his voice in many ways other than crying. His bodily movements are much more controlled and he can roll from his back to his side, kick his legs and push against the foot of his pram or against his mother when she holds him with his feet against her chest. He likes kicking in the bath, too. He likes being taken for a walk in his mother's or father's arms and when his bearer stops walking the baby will make working movements of his body as if to start up the motion again.

He lies awake for longer periods both when put down and after waking up. He will lie on his back in his crib kicking and gurgling and crowing for up to twenty minutes after being fed and before falling asleep.

When he is hungry he will cry and fasten his eyes on his mother's face as she prepares to feed him. He is now friendly and smiling towards other people and shows interest in watching them.

Another critical time for the baby comes when his mother decides it is time to introduce him to solid food. Now he must learn to accept new forms of love and to abandon some of the old. This is a time when his mother or his nurse needs to be sure of herself and her purpose, loving and relaxed. Weaning is not now the dramatic process it used to be, but experts in child health tell us that this period can give rise to many emotional problems. The happy and stable mother may be aware of this although she will not let it worry her or disturb her relationship with her baby. The nurse who is not the baby's mother needs to be thoroughly aware of it and to bring all her skill to the planning and carrying out of weaning (see p. 115).

The baby's greatest need from us now, apart from food and care, is warm approval and our joy in his companionship.

Six months   The baby at six months is growing up fast. He has more than doubled his weight at birth and has grown about five inches longer. He is an interested and interesting member of the family. He has much more control of his body and can wriggle about on his stomach and sit in his pram with a pillow behind him looking about, watching what everyone does, babbling and practising sounds, reaching for his toys and grasping his rattle or a small block or a string of cotton reels, using his whole hand, waving them about and taking them to his mouth to bite and suck. He loves to be on the floor to roll and wriggle, and can sometimes get up on to his hands and knees but cannot quite crawl. He enjoys 'feeling his feet' if we hold his hands and let him pull himself up. His first teeth are nearly ready to erupt and he shows some pleasure in biting rusks and his toys with his hardening gums.

He still swings from contentment to grief and rage quickly if he is not fed soon when he is hungry or if he bumps himself or feels neglected, but he spends much more time awake and alert, content, curious and eager than he did in his early weeks. He watches his mother's face and responds with smiles or anxious looks to her various expressions of pleasure or displeasure.

He loves his mother to play with him, to give him knee-rides, to bounce him on his mattress, to sing to him, to take and give toys. The baby cannot give his mother a toy yet because he still cannot open his grasp to let an object go, but he offers them to her and takes what she offers him. She sings feature and toe games with him and he laughs and chuckles.

He regards strangers now with solemnity and not with delighted smiles as he did when he was three months old. This means that he is beginning to separate those he is most familiar with from those he does not know.

Nine months   The word that springs most easily to mind when we think of the baby at nine months is 'mobile'. At last he can move from place to place and find out what space and distance mean in practice. The baby is now crawling and this is the time when the household must be rearranged so that dangerous things like knives and disinfectants and flexes to electric kettles are put out of his reach and open fires are guarded. Life for his mother is never the same after the baby crawls because she now walks the tightrope of giving him the freedom he needs and keeping him out of danger. He handles everything he can reach and passes things from one hand to another and to his mouth. He may have as many as four teeth now and can bite as well as suck and mouth his toys.

He is increasingly delighted to play with his family and friends, waving, clapping, copying sounds they make to him, laughing, shouting to attract their attention, showing that he recognises familiar gestures and phrases. But he displays growing suspicion of strangers and clings to his mother in their presence.

He needs a number of simple playthings — cotton reels, small bricks, a rag doll, a ball, some small boxes and empty cartons, saucepans and lids, floating toys for his bath.

At this stage the baby is usually having three meals a day. He can hold his mug with both hands and often tries to grasp his spoon. His mother may give him a spoon to himself while she has another one to feed him with.

The nine-month-old is a passionate being, showing delight by eagerly kicking and moving his whole body but showing anger at frustration or at being denied something he wants by stiffening his body and screaming. He is now able to recognise his mother's preparations for bath or meal, and although he shows some impatience if he does not think she is being quick enough he does seem able to wait a little while without too much fuss.

Twelve months   At a year old the baby is a lively member of the family, friendly and confident. He shows less dramatic development in the last three months than during similar periods earlier in his first year but he has consolidated his achievements and is steadily adding to them. He is now constantly pulling himself up by any piece of furniture which lends itself to this and then he moves along by a kind of side-stepping, holding on to the furniture. He can let go and stand alone for a minute. He can walk forwards, his legs wide apart, if we hold his hand. He has several different methods of getting down from a standing position. At first he usually gets down very carefully, hand under hand on the chair or the side of his playpen or whatever he had climbed up against. A little later he abandons the hand work and lets himself down carefully to a squatting position by bending his knees and then flopping on to his behind. But sometimes he gets into the squatting position and then flops forwards on to hands and knees.

He can pick up quite small objects between his thumb and forefinger, and he can now open his hand deliberately to drop things he is holding. This leads to a game of throwing his playthings out of his pram or over the side of his playpen. Of course he enjoys his mother or his other adult friends picking them up and giving them back so he can throw them out again. He learns this way that work brings results!

He watches everything the adults do and copies them exactly, although it is obvious that he does not understand their reasons for doing things.

Emotionally he is a happy, confident, friendly child, no longer so suspicious of strangers, eager to cooperate with anyone who will play voice games, or peep-bo, or ride-a-cock-horse with him. He does fall into a rage when he is frustrated or thwarted but soon recovers because he is so curious about everything that he is easily distracted. He shows little fear of anything but explores confidently, and tirelessly practises over and over feats like getting up and down steps or taking nesting bricks apart.

He can play alone happily if he knows his mother is not far away but welcomes his mother and father after short absences with a crow, a shout, a laugh or some movement such as jerking his whole body, rapid crawling or burrowing into his pillow with shouts of joy.

He uses his voice ceaselessly, chattering long 'sentences' to himself, burring, lalling, crowing, imitating noises around him — even to the cry of a shrill bird in the garden, or the squeak of his rubber toys. He can say one or two distinct syllables such as 'dad-dad' and 'mum-mum-mum' which he uses often, but he understands many more words than he can say, especially if his mother has always talked to him about what she is doing so that he recognises words like 'bath' and 'dinner'. He obeys simple requests like 'Give it to Mummy' if they are accompanied by a gesture.

He greets dogs rapturously at this age but his attitude to other children is one of mild curiosity. Here is a description of the meeting of two little girls, B. aged one year one month and R. aged eleven months.

R. was taken to visit B. She accepted the new surroundings calmly and crawled round the house exploring. Looked with interest at B. when she was brought in but soon turned her attention to B.'s toys. B. was very much interested in R. and began handing her various toys which R. pushed away without looking at them, her attention being directed to a toy monkey made of fur. Later B. pushed and poked R. who made no effort to retaliate and only cried once when B. hit her sharply on the head with a metal cigarette case. Later, however, R. was put to rest in a pram on the verandah with a chair beside it. B. was heard to scream suddenly and was found standing on the chair looking at R. who was sitting up. On B.'s finger were deep marks of R.'s teeth. Later both were sitting on the floor and B.

was rubbing her open hand over R.'s face. R. had her mouth open and was trying to bite B.'s palm. B. showed much more active social behaviour than R. throughout the day, although R. showed definite interest in B. At one time B. knocked two cushions from a window seat on to the floor and began burrowing into one of them. R. crawled over and began burrowing into the other.

At this time of his life the baby needs a great deal of freedom to crawl, stand and try to walk so we must provide safe space for him. A playpen is not large enough and should only be used when his mother is cooking or gardening or entertaining visitors, and then the playpen should be put where the baby can watch her and call to her.

He wants his parents to play with him and this means that they must be willing to give him their time and active cooperation and encouragement. Periods of the undivided attention of mother or father are worth more to the child now and for the next three years than any number of expensive toys.

The second year

This is a year of exploration and discovery on two fronts — the physical world and the world of language and speech. For the first half of his second year the little child is urgently concerned with mastering the skill of walking, balancing, picking things up and carrying them about. He builds up his ability to control his environment by exploring it ceaselessly and testing it out in every way he can and when he has got to the stage of walking about freely, climbing on to sofas and chairs, negotiating stairs and pushing and pulling his play material about, he launches his energies into experimenting with speech. For over a year he has been practising and imitating all kinds of sounds, listening to grown-ups talking, storing up in his mind the names of the most familiar objects in his surroundings and enjoying the rhythm of sentences, songs and rhymes. Now, at about eighteen months, he is ready to enter this exciting world of communication. This is a vital step, for without language he cannot go much further in thinking and reasoning and learning. The loving adults in the life of the fortunate baby have been talking and singing to him ever since he was born, but now he needs their help even more. The baby in an inarticulate home and the baby whose parents or guardians are too busy to talk to him are at a serious disadvantage at this critical stage of development.

Fifteen months   The little child between his first and second birth-days plunges out to meet life with open arms, and at fifteen months he is full of confidence in himself and wants everyone to be aware of him and his exploits. He is possessive of his mother and jealous of anything which takes her attention from him. He does not object to her going about her household tasks because he can follow her about and 'help' but he at once resents her taking up a book to read, or sitting down to write letters or to sew and pulls at her arm or tries to climb on to her lap. He may even sit down and knock his head on the floor between his knees and cry in a self-conscious manner to draw attention to himself. He enjoys trying to be independent about feeding himself, exploring, playing alone, walking unaided and pushing his push-chair along but at the same time he likes his mother to be within easy reach and he follows her about a good deal, cries if he loses her for long and puts up his arms to be lifted up when he finds her again. He is fairly cooperative about being dressed — putting his arms through sleeves and holding out his feet for shoes and socks — but he does not like dressing to take too long. He usually thoroughly enjoys his bath, especially if he is given plenty of time to play with floating toys and soap dishes and brushes and allowed to investigate the taps and the plug. He does not like being frustrated or denied what he wants and tends to scream but it is easy to distract him with a new interest.

He spends most of his time relentlessly exploring, discovering, experimenting with everything he can find. He may scream or squeal with rage when he cannot manage something he wants to do such as put on a shoe or push blocks through the bars of his playpen. He frequently flings away the offending article but nearly always returns to it and tries again. He examines everything he can reach but for the most part he does not spend a great deal of time on any one object, he likes to go on to the next interesting thing. The activities he enjoys most with his playthings are ones in which he can drop things into boxes or empty cartons and tip them out again. For instance he loves putting cotton reels or conkers or wooden cubes into empty breakfast cereal cartons. He also likes to put nesting blocks or beakers inside one another and often gets the order right. He still likes to have several saucepans and their lids to play with. He likes a rag doll or animal to throw around and he likes to push boxes and his little chair or a horse on wheels for a little while. He will roll a ball along but usually prefers to put it in a basket or a shopping bag or a saucepan. He does not usually take things to his mouth to investigate them as he used to do but now mainly feels them and turns them round with his hands.

Many mothers begin in earnest at this stage to introduce the child to a pot. He has not yet got control of his bowels and bladder but can now understand the use of the lavatory because he is aware of the adults' use of it and so it is a sensible time to suggest he will soon use a pot. The mother is matter-of-fact about it and makes no comment if the child is uninterested. Any success with use of a pot at this stage is likely to be due to the judgement of the mother who sees signs of imminent movement of bowels or bladder.

The baby is too much interested in his increasing success at walking to pay much attention yet to his vocabulary. But he talks to himself in long sentences of gibberish as he plays and makes most expressive noises. Frequently he says a long 'sentence' and answers himself by a definite 'yes'. He is sometimes heard practising definite words and he uses a large range of inflexion. He understands a good deal of what is said to him and he uses a few words economically. He is clever at making one word express several ideas. For instance, 'Ta' is used by the same child at different times to mean 'Thank you' or 'Please give me that' or 'Here, you can have this one'; and 'Ta-ta' or 'Bye-bye' is used to mean 'Goodbye' or 'Let us go for a walk' or 'Go away, I don't want you here'.

Eighteen months   By the time he is halfway through his second year he is fairly steady on his feet and becomes more independent in his excursions about the house. He is curious and eager and opens cupboards and drawers, pulling the contents out, tipping and spilling and turning things over. He tries to turn knobs and shakes anything that rattles or is loose. He can bear to be out of sight of his mother for a little longer and although he likes to imitate her and other adults he is not as cooperative as he was earlier about such things as dressing and eating. He flies into a fury at frustration of any kind and is often obstinate and contrary. His rage is not only directed towards adults who inhibit him, but also towards the nature of the material he is trying to work with. A mother writes about her little girl at this age:

> She often insists on pushing her push-chair when we are out walking and this afternoon she pushed it up a steep hill by one hand, crying and sobbing bitterly all the way up but seemingly obsessed with the necessity to do it. She screamed with rage whenever I attempted to help her. It was a big feat of strength and she only took two very brief pauses. She has recently been given a wheeled horse and has great fun with it. Sometimes she becomes obsessed and overexcited with it and screams and sobs

when it gets jammed into a corner or against a piece of furniture but at other times she patiently backs and turns it.

Now he becomes intensely interested in talking and his vocabulary grows fast, so that by his second birthday he may be using between 50 and 200 words. He very much enjoys games with his parents in which features and parts of the body are named and he can usually point to each part when asked to do so. He repeats a good many words after the adult. Well before he is two years old he may be putting two words together. For instance, instead of just saying 'No' when milk too warm is offered to him he will now say 'No, 'ot'. He recognises pictures of people and animals as 'Daddy', 'bubba', ''orse' or 'wow-wow', and may say two words as he points to them – 'See, birdie', or 'bubba socks'.

It is at this stage that the baby needs his parents and friends to talk to him constantly, naming things they are working with, describing what they are doing, discussing the traffic, looking at pictures with him, all in short clear sentences because he can't cope with a flow of words. He picks words out and repeats them and practises them to himself. Sometimes when he is excited or wants the adults' approval he will run off his whole vocabulary in a stream – 'Light, fire, bus, dear Daddy, 'orse, baba', and so on.

Although parents and guardians find this second year an exhausting one for them because the baby's energy seems far greater than their own, it is also an exciting one because he makes such strides in his development and by the end of it seems no longer to be a baby but has emerged as an independent, confident young child.

The third year

This is often a mixed year of storms and tantrums, anxieties, imaginative fears, nightmares, together with delightful progress towards independence, sunny periods of confidence and happy companionship and rapidly growing ability to communicate ideas and feelings and to ask for information.

The child at two is sturdy and energetic. He weighs about 11.7 kg (26 lb) and is about 81 cm (32 inches) high. He runs about easily, although he is a little wary if older, more boisterous children are about, and he climbs on to furniture and up and down stairs quite easily. He spends a good deal of time following his mother and other friendly adults about and copies what they do, with much more understanding of their purpose than he had a year ago. He can brush up the dust his mother sweeps but he does not do it very well and although she thanks him cheerfully she has to do it again when he is not there to see. He likes to do things in the same way every time and to have his mother follow the same routine every day.

He is loving and responsive but increasingly shows that he has a will of his own and tries very hard to be independent. This often leads to frustrations and clashes with adults over necessary inhibitions. He says 'No' a good deal and may frequently fall into tantrums. These temper tantrums during the day are closely related to the nightmares he often has at night at this age. He may often wake screaming with fear and needs to be comforted and reassured. The dark frightens him, too, and sometimes animals, even dogs he has known for months, may become fearsome to him.

It is difficult for us completely to understand the child's fears at this time. One thing for us to bear in mind is that he is still in the stage of being wholly possessed by whatever emotion he feels at the moment so that when he feels angry rage boils up in him till he feels bursting with it and this is not at all a comfortable feeling. It begins to terrify him although he means it to terrify us towards whom it is directed. Another thing we must remember is that at this age the little child knows nothing about scientific principles or about cause and effect. He knows he feels powerful emotions and he believes that they are so powerful that they cause things to happen. If he is angry and violent towards his mother and she goes off suddenly leaving him with a neighbour and does not come back for some time he feels it is his doing — she went away because he was angry with her. He does not know that a telephone call has summoned her to a sudden illness of his grandmother. Opportunities for this kind of misunderstanding must often happen in residential nurseries where, even though the children are in small family groups, the staff must have defined hours of duty and seem to the children to be coming and going a good deal. If sometimes the going off duty of a member of staff coincides with an outburst of rage on the part of the child towards her, he may feel frightened and guilty. His anger must have sent her away and she may never come back.

This is yet another thing we have to try to understand — that his angry feelings and aggressive acts towards people he loves dearly and whom he wants to love him make the child miserable and guilty. We know ourselves how unhappy we feel when we have been rude or ill-tempered to those we love and we are sophisticated people, knowledgeable about the general principles of how the world works. How much worse it must seem to the child who does not yet know that his feelings and impulses are not in some way magic and may cause awful things to happen. In the same way he does not yet know that the terrifying experiences he has in nightmares are not real. His experience of life is so very much limited that he is not yet aware of the difference between what is dream and what is reality.

So we must be careful of our behaviour towards the little child in a temper. In the first place we should try to avoid outbursts whenever possible by making our demands on him reasonable and the daily routine we plan for him as free as possible from frustrating situations. We do have to inhibit him — to stop his play for meals and bath and bed, to put certain places and things out of bounds, to take him shopping and not let him run into the road — but we can cut these inhibitions to a minimum if we set our minds to understand his needs. Then we can often forestall an outburst by recognising that the circumstances are building up in that direction and either altering the situation or distracting him by suggesting a fresh occupation.

When a tantrum does happen we must realise that the child needs help. We may not be able to lift him and comfort him if he is kicking and screaming on the floor (for instance it may be difficult for a pregnant mother) but we can remain calm and wait close by until he feels better. It only makes things much worse if we fly into a rage as well because then we show him that we can't control ourselves and are therefore not likely to be able to control him. This will frighten him more than ever because however much he attacks us he needs to know that we can set bounds for his fury, and not let him destroy us and himself.

I should like to say a word here about our being cross with the child, or, indeed, with other people in his presence. Of course we are sometimes cross and irritable and show it, and this does the child no harm. In fact it reassures him to find that we can be angry and still remain in control of ourselves because then he can believe that he will be able to do the same. It is when we fly into an uncontrolled rage that he is quite rightly terrified.

Although the child is often miserable because of his struggle with loving and hating us at the same time, it would be a sign of danger if he were not unhappy about it. Being unhappy means that he does care about us and does not want to hurt us. If he had no concern for us he would not feel guilty and anxious. If he is not concerned about us then he is not making the human bonds that will let him become a healthy social being.

But the two-year-old is not a cross, contrary child for more than part of the time — he is eager and curious and affectionate. He talks almost all the time and his 'Whazzat?' echoes in his parents' ears long after he goes to bed — his ceaseless asking for the names of things and people. His vocabulary grows rapidly. He loves to hear simple stories, fingerplays, songs and rhymes. He begins to use sentences of three or four words and before his third birthday he is referring to himself as 'I'.

He loves to dress up in hats and shoes and pretend to be a grown-up, copying adult actions minutely. He should have sand and water to play with now and he also needs dolls and shawls to wrap them in, boxes, bricks, a cart or box on wheels, balls, tins, cartons, cotton reels, hammer pegs, posting boxes, material such as buttons and postcards which he can sort into piles and put into boxes. He watches other children and is happy to play near them, even with the same sort of play material, but he rarely plays with them or shares his toys. Sometimes he allows himself to be used as a baby or a sick child in the dramatic games of older chilren. If we are responsible for a group of several two-year-olds we find that we must provide a good many of the same kinds of toys — several dolls, several boxes or carts, a number of bricks, two or three balls, because they like the same playthings but do not know how to take turns.

Towards the end of this third year the little child becomes less self-willed and more amenable to adult suggestion. He is still eager and curious but more willing to fall in with what his parents want him to do.

The fourth year

By his third birthday some of the troublesome things of babyhood have been overcome. The child has control of his bowels and of his bladder during the daytime at least. He may still wet his bed and of course if he is overtired or anxious or ill he may have accidents during the day. Teething is also over for the time being. He usually has his full set of milk teeth by the time he is about two-and-a-half. His body works easily and well now and he can climb and run and jump confidently. About his third birthday he finds he can ride a tricycle and throw a ball. He is not yet expert in the finer movements of hand and finger muscles, but he scribbles and draws with pencils and crayons quite satisfactorily and can soon cut with scissors. He paints now, if he is given the opportunity, using wide sweeping movements of his arm, so he needs big pieces of paper and thick brushes.

He is now talking freely, exchanging greetings and news, asking for information, telling about his own adventures. He asks innumerable questions, mostly beginning with 'what' or 'where' or 'who'. He collects new words enthusiastically all the time.

This is the stage in his development when the child not only copies the gestures and actions of the grown-ups around him but also adopts their attitudes to life. If his parents are pleasant, helpful, responsible, loving people, these are the attitudes he will take for his own. If, on the other hand, they are greedy, selfish and bullying he will most likely become greedy and selfish and a bully himself. These attitudes are betrayed in intangible as well as overt ways by the adults and are extremely contagious. The child is now ready to 'catch' them.

He is also ready for another big step in his social development. The time is ripe for him to enjoy the companionship of other children. If his relationships with adults have been satisfying up to now he is ready to move on to make good relationships with children of his own age. If he has brothers and sisters not too much older or younger he will have enjoyed their company in many ways before this. Babies of six months onwards love to play with older brothers and sisters, and mothers describe many instances of joyful games with the baby copying the older child and great tenderness and affection shown to the baby by the two- or three-year-old.

With the opportunity to be with other children of his own age he soon discovers that his game is more fun if another child joins him. If he wants a plaything the other child has he is more likely to get it if he gives the other child something of his. It is not that our child is suddenly unselfish and benevolent towards the others. He is still basically bent on satisfying himself but he soon realises that others will join in his play if they are satisfied too, and that it is worth giving as well as taking and even waiting a bit while others have their turn.

Now is the time when the fortunate three-year-old joins a play-group or a nursery school for a few hours each day. Dr Blurton Jones formerly of the Department of Growth and Development, Institute of Child Health, London, describes what he calls rough and tumble play among nursery school children.[1] He says this kind of play, where children chase each other, wrestle, jump up and down in front of each other, laughing, and beat at each other with open hands or with objects without actually hitting the other child, although to some adults it appears hostile, is not in fact aggressive but a friendly form of play which, he suggests, is important in the social development of the children. He has observed that most children

[1] Some aspects of the social behaviour of children in nursery school in *Primate Ethology*, ed. D. Morris, Weidenfeld & Nicolson, 1966.

take part in rough and tumble play, though boys do so more than girls. Some few children do not join in the usual activities of the others and do not take part in rough and tumble play. Dr Blurton Jones has observed signs of rough and tumble play in children as young as eighteen months and wonders whether there is 'a critical period for developing the ability to rough and tumble' and that these solitary children have passed it before they came to nursery school or had an opportunity to play with others at home. This is an interesting suggestion and the observations of teachers and assistants in nurseries could make valuable contributions to greater knowledge of the whole subject.

Three-year-olds spend a good deal of time in imaginative and dramatic play, and they also project their own experiences on to their playthings: any experiences which have puzzled, disturbed or interested them are worked over and dramatised in their play, and their dolls and animals often play leading roles. 'My little baby has a sore throat', says the child putting his soft toy to bed. Sensible adults do not show dismay when they see a child beating or stamping on her doll because they realise that she knows the doll is not a real baby and is using it as a safety valve for aggressive feelings and that this is normal behaviour for this stage of her development. Imaginative play can be solitary but it becomes more elaborate, with more children joining in, as the children find satisfaction in sharing and cooperating.

Another advantage to the child who goes to a nursery school or playgroup is that he meets friendly and helpful adults outside his home and family circle. The fact that such adults exist is a reassurance to him — the outside world can also love and value him. Because nursery school teachers are trained and understand a good deal about young children they know how much children need to be thought strong, useful and lovable and they take each child as he is, with his own abilities and attainments and temperament, and accept him gladly for himself. It is, of course, important that parents and the staff of the nursery school or playgroup should work together for the good of the child because if these two sets of powerful adults in his world are at cross purposes the child is bewildered and confused. This first step away from home and mother must not take him into anxiety or insecurity or its critical value is lost, and when later he goes to school, as he must, he may be apprehensive and suspicious.

The three-year-old is a happy and companionable child, who needs opportunities for independence, play with many different materials, time to be with other children, a great deal of conversation and story-telling, and the support and example of affectionate, reliable adults.

The four-year-old

The four-year-old child is more boisterous than the three-year-old. He is energetic and confident, physically agile, inventive and independent. He is on the whole a reasonable being. He likes to know the reasons for adult demands but he responds to sensible direction. He has by now some standards by which to judge his own behaviour and that of other people. He can criticise other children and does not hesitate to criticise adults, whom he expects to abide by their own rules. 'You didn't wash your hands' he will point out to an adult who takes a book from the shelf. Everyone knows you are expected to have clean hands before you look at books!

In his play the four-year-old shows that he can plan ahead and work with an end in view. This shows clearly in some of the big building projects which go on in nursery schools with groups of four-year-olds. He can control his emotions fairly well and often shows a remarkable amount of patience in working out a practical problem or learning to manipulate some new piece of material.

The four-year-olds tend to play in groups, particularly in their imaginative and building play. These groups often break up and re-form with different children, but many children have constant companions with whom they are especially friendly and with whom they do most things together. Leaders stand out clearly in many of these groups, and there is apparent a wide variety of personalities among the children. This is clearer than among younger groups — the character of the four-year-old seems to have 'set' already.

In the nursery school or playgroup the four-year-old children do not seek the active companionship of the teachers and assistants in their play. They ask for material they need, or sometimes for advice; they go to an adult for help when they are hurt; they like to have an adult's approval of something they have made or painted; they cheerfully respond to most reasonable adult requests and reminders; and they sometimes need adults to arbitrate in disputes. But on the whole they are happy to play together, with the adults as a reliable background. Children of this age are concerned for each other and will tell an adult when another child is in trouble or take a hurt child to her. A four-year-old who is new to the nursery may stay close to the teacher or to an assistant for some days, investigating a little further afield each day until he is absorbed in the activities of the others, but he usually does not need this closeness to an adult for as long as a new three-year-old does.

One real need children have for adults at this age is to answer questions. By this time the child has marshalled a good deal of information and now wants reasons and so he asks a great many questions beginning with 'why', and he wants proper answers.

He is still struggling with fact and fantasy and is fond of telling long and elaborate stories about his own doings, many of which are purely imaginary. Some parents worry about his flights of fancy but the nursery school staff usually enter into the fun and by good-humoured questioning help him to prune his tale to fit facts or laugh with him at its absurd details.

Between four-and-a-half and five the child often seems to change. Some children become over-confident, noisy, rude and silly. The girls snigger and mince about and are impertinent, the boys swagger and swear and shout and are deliberately disobedient. There may be several reasons for this change. The child feels himself to be growing up and becoming independent of adult control; he feels strong and capable and resents being treated as a baby. Another reason is that he may be bored. At home he has probably exhausted most of the possibilities of house and garden and wants wider horizons; he needs more to do. In the nursery school, especially if he has been there for over a year, he needs to be extended. The play material seems stale and the activities undemanding, so he rebels and becomes un-cooperative. The understanding staff of a good nursery school recognise symptoms and unobtrusively suggest new ways of using familiar material, introduce challenging new tools and equipment, especially designed for the use of the nearly-fives, make the music and story periods more interesting, have more advanced books in a special place, take the child further afield occasionally to visit places like fire stations and building sites, and give some real responsibilities such as care for a pet, or bringing in the milk, or mopping up the bathroom floor.

Another possible reason for his trying behaviour at nearly five may be that he knows he will be starting 'real' school soon. He has been told about it and older children discuss school in his hearing. Although he longs to be grown-up and recognises that going to school is a definite step in this direction, anxiety is mixed with excitement. This happens to us all, all through our lives once we are old enough to anticipate the next step. We long for the new oppor-tunity but shrink from leaving the known, familiar life of the present. The nursery school or the playgroup has been a successful first step away from home but 'big' school is a bigger step into a less sheltered world. No wonder this mixture of feelings disturbs the child. It must be even more an anxiety to the child who has not had the experience of the playgroup or nursery school and to whom other children of his own age are still an unknown factor.

The five-year-old

The years from five to eight form a bridge between the early period of rapid development and the later period of slower growth before puberty. They are interesting years, full of the excitement of fresh discovery, of widening boundaries and of pleasure in mastering new material. It is a time of weaning, too, because the child in these years is gradually taking on responsibility for his own life and depending less and less on adult support.

The five-year-old is a sturdy, agile child, usually energetic and lively. He does not grow as fast as he did in his first four years but he changes bodily shape. He still, at his fifth birthday, has the proportions of babyhood — the large head, short legs and rounded contours, but these soon begin to change. His head grows very little bigger but his legs grow longer so that he soon has more nearly the proportions of an adult. His face loses the baby pads of fat and the features are more pronounced so that family likenesses often show clearly at this age. His voice is still high, and during play or when he is excited it is shrill, but it tends to become lower and more controlled as he goes about his work at school.

Most five-year-olds are confident and friendly. They expect to be liked and valued and they are ready to go out to meet new experiences. They are eager to learn and to please the adults. They talk readily and ask a great many questions, particularly 'why?', and they show a surprising amount of persistence when they want to master some new skill. They can control their emotions fairly well especially in pursuit of their own purposes; they find that impatience and bad temper hinder them in what they are trying to do.

They work and play with each other in small groups, but each five-year-old is really interested most of all in himself and what he wants to do. He realises that the other children are useful to his ends and he is willing to be useful to theirs in exchange but children of this age are rivals rather than collaborators. For this reason they are not interested in team games as these are understood by children a few years older. They concentrate hard on skills they want to master like skipping with a rope, using a scooter, riding a bicycle, reading or using a screwdriver. They like games in which each can excel, so they do a good many things like seeing who can hop longest on one foot or run fastest round the lawn. We often see a group of five-year-olds together running about, jumping, bouncing, turning somersaults, accompanied by much laughter and by shrill cries, but it is not really a group activity, each child is performing to himself in the company of others. He thoroughly enjoys being with them and their exploits urge him on to try new and more daring feats, but he does not see himself as a member of a team.

On the other hand, two children at this age will often play together very successfully. A mother writes:

> I am amazed at how differently Maggie plays with different children. When Emily comes they play for the whole afternoon quietly, constructively and with much imagination. The floor is covered with improvised beds for all the dolls and soft toys, a tea table is elaborately laid out using all sorts of things for dishes and food and they talk all the time about what they are doing in low voices, completely absorbed. But when Martha comes she and Maggie seem to do nothing but rush madly about all over the house, shrieking and laughing, treating the toys carelessly and breaking rules with a kind of giggling defiance. For instance, I find them climbing the shelves in the airing cupboard which they know is forbidden but it is as if they want me to find them and be cross. They love to hide from me and the other grown-ups, and they are rather good at this, hiding very quietly for a long time. When we take too long to find them they begin to giggle.

Five-year-olds are sometimes boastful and seem to show off a good deal. Some adults find this annoying and tiresome but experienced teachers know it is a natural outcome of their self-confidence and cope with it by matter-of-fact good humour and encouragement of the children's real achievements. Too much showing-off, however, may mean that the child is lacking confidence, perhaps because he has not been given enough things to do for himself or not shown how to go about learning new skills. He needs more opportunities, material and help so that he can achieve more. Then genuine praise and encouragement will make boasting unnecessary. Most five-year-olds embroider facts about their exploits and their family's doings. Reality and fantasy are still mixed up in their minds and what they would like to have done is often muddled with what they actually did.

Children of this age like and trust grown-ups and although they like to be independent they do in fact depend a great deal on adults for organisation, help and advice and as arbiters in the wrangles that inevitably spring up among a group of rivals. Parents and teachers are responsible for the planning and organisation of home and classroom

within which the ᵁ...   ...leas often expand from
the play and work of the

Five-year-olds are ᵣ...   ... things; they are very
matter-of-fact. As a rul... ... e dark much and they are
certainly afraid of be⁰ ... ...ve bad dreams they may
wake up frightened an... ... describe what frightened
them because, half-asleep... ...ieir language is not up to
it, so they need comforting ...—... uch discussion. One real
danger of this age group is that they are not enough afraid of traffic.
This is because they have no experience of how to control a vehicle
and no comprehension of relative speeds and their immediate
impulses are so strong (to join a friend on the other side of the road;
to get an ice-cream; to recover a ball) that they take no account of
the hazards. Traffic often excites rather than frightens them.

The biggest change that comes into the life of the five-year-old is
that he goes to school. Even in countries where the legal age of entry
to school is six years the five-year-old often enters kindergarten. The
change from home life is challenging, sometimes frightening, but
exciting and rewarding. His horizons are widened and new relationships formed. If his parents have brought him up to have confidence
he will accept and enjoy school quickly. He accepts his teacher as a
mother figure but soon learns he has to share her attention and
affection with all the other children. But he also finds that he has
others to like, to have fun with, to share with and to imitate. This
last is important. It is a good thing that he should have a variety of
models to copy so that he can decide what behaviour he admires and
what standards he wants to accept. His basic standards are those he
has unconsciously absorbed from his parents, but these can be
modified and adapted to his own emerging personality. The new
relationships he forms at school allow a diffusion of his emotional
pressures which is healthy and something of a release from the
intense feelings he has within the family. The teacher's discipline is
more impersonal than that of his parents, and the other children
exert a social pressure because he wants their good opinion. The
child who has been to a playgroup or a nursery school has already
met this situation and can give his attention more quickly to the
other interesting things of school.

By the time the five-year-old enters school his personality is
becoming well defined, so much so that the staff at school can
recognise and plan round it, since they try to adapt the environment
of school to each child's needs and abilities. They see that one child
is a potential leader, another is a steady stayer, another an imaginative dreamer, another is timid and needs help to build up confidence

in himself, this little girl will quietly mother the shy ones, this one is bossy, and this one is insecure and will flit from one occupation to another unless they can capture her real interest.

However prepared he is for the new life the child will be tired for the first days or even weeks of school and needs extra attention from his mother when he reaches home. Mothers report that some of the things that worry children for the first weeks of school are where to find things, changing shoes and clothing in the time given, finding and using strange lavatories, being bossed by a well-meaning child, not understanding the teacher's accent and being left out of things by the other children. The five-year-old likes to conform and can't bear to be rejected by his peers. He also thinks that rules are absolute and must on no account be broken, so he may be really frightened of terrible consequences if he makes a mistake about where to put his coat or his paintbrushes. These troubles soon clear up, especially if his mother and his teacher tackle them together and he is reassured if mother and teacher like and respect each other. He is fundamentally a loving and trusting child. When he is happy and occupied he is independent and confident, but when he is overtired or unhappy or sick he easily becomes a baby again and turns to the trusted adult for comfort and help.

The six-year-old

By their sixth birthday children are friendly, trusting and coopera-tive towards adults, intensely interested and curious about the world, lively and energetic. They grow steadily, their bodies now slim and flexible. They begin to lose their milk teeth at about this time and this excites them because it is a sign that they are growing up but at the same time there is some apprehension at losing a bit of themselves. Some find it funny to speak through the gap, others feel shy at the effect it has on their speech. The child's normal tone of voice is lower than at five years but it rises to shrill when he is excited or is demanding attention. He talks clearly and well if he is encouraged to do so. His appetite varies from day to day about this time — on some days he seems hardly interested in food, on others he eats well.

His muscular control is improving and he likes to run on tiptoe, skip and dance in time to music. He is competent with pencils and paintbrushes, can control a large needle or a pair of knitting needles fairly well, can dress himself even though he is rather slow about it, is able to use the lavatory by himself (although some children still like some help), and works hard to master things like using stilts and roller-skates (Elizabeth screamed at her father who offered help 'I know *what* to do, I just don't know *how* to do it'). He is restless and seems always to be on the move except when he is concentrating on work or experiment, when he can be still and absorbed for a long time.

One thing that often irritates adults with six-year-olds is that they still have little idea of time passing. They are so curious and interested in everything that they appear to be 'dawdling and messing-about' when the grown-up expects them to be 'getting on' with a job. The fact is that the six-year-old appears to be so competent and sensible that we expect him to be more mature than he really is. We must remember, too, that we often waste his time. We sometimes keep him waiting for us in an exasperating way. We may be just about to do something or to go somewhere with him when the telephone rings or a colleague comes up with a question and we spend time answering while he has to wait, his eagerness draining away.

Willing as he is to try out new experiences the six-year-old usually likes the adults to be in the background. For instance I took a young friend, just six, into a shop which was new to her and as I bought vegetables at one counter I suggested she buy an ice-cream at another. She went to the counter but hesitated and I said, 'Would you like me to buy it?' She replied, 'No, I'll do it but you stay here.'

Six-year-olds have a great interest in reality. They ask constantly 'Is it true?' Their fantasy play has strong elements of real life in it, copying adult behaviour for the most part, and showing evidence of careful observation. Dramatic play now begins to turn into drama — that is to say, although they dress up and play different roles they like to have a coherent story running through the play and they like other children and adults to watch.

A girl and her brother, eighteen months younger, whom I know well, had for some time talked about a group of imaginary companions they had, known as 'boyfriends', who had all kinds of adventures and could do marvellous things. At about the time Claudia went to school Oliver's fantasy friends coalesced into one imaginary creature called Fiery Boyfriend Dragon, and both children talked a great deal about him. But by the time Claudia was six she was saying to Oliver 'He didn't *really* do that', or, 'He doesn't *really* go there', so that one day when I asked Oliver about Fiery Boyfriend Dragon he looked self-conscious, threw himself into my arms and said 'I'm afraid he isn't quite true'. He wasn't convinced but Claudia's nagging efforts to disentangle fact from fancy were making him have doubts.

At this age they are also beginning to question their earlier belief that unbreakable rules govern life. They ask 'Why?' more and more urgently. Margaret (six) watched her grandfather take a pill and said 'Do you swallow it whole?' 'Yes.' 'Why do you have to?' The form of her last question shows how her mind was working. Was this way of taking pills a rule of life and if so, why?

The six-year-old is not frightened of many things but he is more nervous of imaginary situations than the five-year-old — of being held by robbers, chased by witches, haunted by ghosts, involved with creatures from space. Two young neighbours aged six and seven used to come to watch Dr Who on my television. They watched it standing on armchairs, looking over the backs of the chairs so that when it got too frightening they could crouch down and hide till it sounded safer. They liked me to sit and watch with them. I asked them why they watched it when they hid so much of the time but they said 'Everybody does', and that seemed to be an unanswerable argument. When he has nightmares, however, the six-year-old can talk about it more clearly with his parents and this helps to dissipate his fear.

Because the six-year-old is so curious and so much interested in everything he enjoys the work of the first school into which he has now become absorbed. A good school suits him perfectly. It gives him ample opportunities to collect facts and learn new skills and lets him work at his own pace. It is important to him at this stage to do this because he needs to ponder over some things, to take time to puzzle other things out, to practise this and that till he is sure he has it mastered, and then to forge ahead rapidly for a while. He is eager to learn and if the school gives him all the help he needs his mastery of methods and materials makes him able to trust himself and to go on by himself. He grows gradually less dependent on adults for companionship and emotional satisfaction, and finds these in his mates. He can plan and carry out schemes of work with trusted companions and they learn together how to make their separate contributions to the project. It is at this stage that earlier experience of manipulating material pays off because we can see many evidences of his reasoning stemming from knowledge he has discovered for himself. For instance, a classroom assistant reports:

> One of our six-year-old boys tried to look over the school wall. He wasn't tall enough so he found a piece of wood and leant it against the wall. He ran up the wood but it slipped down so he looked around, found a piece of brick, wedged it just under the wood and was able to walk up and look over the wall.

and a mother writes:

> Two four-year-old boys and a six-year-old girl were looking

through a glossy magazine at home. They came to a picture which was very dark and the two boys said they couldn't see the picture properly. One boy said 'It's because it's dark in the room, let's put the light on' (it was really quite light in the room). The girl said, 'It won't make any difference to the picture.' The boys took no notice of her and put the light on. They were surprised that it made no difference to the picture. They then got a torch and kept shining it at the picture from different angles. Eventually they gave up and said, 'You were right, Mandy, it is a dark picture.'

As the year goes on towards his seventh birthday we can see the six-year-old becoming less dependent on his parents and putting more weight on his teacher's opinions and what he does with his classmates. He becomes more critical of himself too, and is able to some extent to stand off from his own work and appraise it. He is possessive about his possessions and tools and is sometimes irritable and annoyed when they are touched or borrowed without his express permission. He still likes to do well and to be praised but at home he is less cooperative and is sometimes silly, screaming with idiot laughter and trying out jokes, riddles and word puzzles aimed at his parents. He often gets the jokes wrong but he enjoys this harmless form of defiance. He may ignore rules about hanging up his clothes or washing his hands at home although at school he likes obeying the rules. He may sometimes refuse to help with the usual small chores at home while at school he enjoys working and only resents his teacher when she doesn't work him hard enough.

The groups he plays with at school grow bigger and it is unusual to find a six-year-old playing by himself. To be rejected by the other children is dreadful to him. Much of the playground activity still seems to the adults to be running about, huddling in groups, chasing and scuffling. They seem to make up their own rules ('When I put my hand over my mouth you can't catch me'). Indoors the play is mostly constructive. They enjoy construction sets and making things. They paint with confidence and their paintings are of fairly recognisable people, animals, buildings, vehicles, often showing details of surprising accuracy such as the door fastening on a van or the angle of the wings on an aircraft. Human figures usually have hands with fingers. They experiment with collage and printing, making patterns and modelling. Sex differences show in some of their play. The boys collect and play with model cars, trains and road vehicles and most girls play with dolls or puppets or animals, or they play houses. The models must be good representations of real trains and vehicles with the main details correct and the dolls must have well-made clothes, beds and prams. The girls will join in a well-organised or adult-shared game with the train sets and model cars but at this age the boys rarely play with dolls. Girls are quite skilful at skipping with a rope but boys on the whole are better at throwing and catching balls. Both boys and girls like climbing and swinging, kicking balls about and trying to hit them with bats and sticks.

At parties they are quite prepared to accept adult direction and games like: 'Pinning the tail on the donkey'; 'Pass the parcel'; 'Hunt the thimble'; 'Simon says'; 'Statues'; and 'Spin the plate' are nearly always successful. These games can, with careful planning, be played so that no one has to drop out and they give everyone a chance to shine. 'Oranges and lemons' and 'Did you ever see a lassie (laddie)?' are favourite singing games as long as they don't go on too long. A treasure hunt outside is usually much enjoyed but it needs a garden without too many precious plants.

This is the time when some children are at a disadvantage and begin to slip backwards at school, unable to keep up with the rest, the gap between their pace and that of the others widening steadily. They are children of parents uninterested in learning or even hostile to school; children from families who do not communicate with each other in words or from immigrant families whose command and understanding of English is poor; children from other parts of the country where accents and habits of life may be different so that they find it difficult to grasp what is going on; or children from homes so poor that they are overcome with exhaustion, bad health, anxiety or even fear and cannot learn. Their teacher may be aware of the situation but because of the numbers of children she has to cope with, or the lack of cooperation of parents or her own lack of insight or experience she is not able to do much to help.

On the other hand this is also the time when some intelligent children from disadvantaged homes seize on the riches that school offers and find in life at school all that makes up for difficulties at home. Other problems of jealousy and hostility may arise out of this situation. Whatever the reason, when home and school do not work together the child suffers.

The seven-year-old

By the time he is in his eighth year the child has a good grasp of fact as distinct from fantasy. He has spent more than two years, with the help of his teachers, working at discovering in an orderly way how things work and behave, and he is naturally a practical being at this stage so his imaginative play centres around practical situations and begins to give way to dramatic play in the adult sense, where the participants know themselves to be acting roles. He likes stories about real people who do brave and clever things or about powerful people who overcome great odds.

Once he can read the child is heir to the stored knowledge of man and he should be encouraged both to find out for himself and to refer to books. This means that a rich and stimulating environment is necessary for him at home and at school. At seven he can use materials which require finer hand movements than when he was five and so he finds a good deal of pleasure in building with Meccano and Lego, and in train sets, or in using finer brushes for painting; girls especially begin to enjoy sewing and knitting. Children of this age sometimes spend periods of time working by themselves at activities of this kind. But they also spend a lot of time climbing and running, balancing, throwing and dancing. They now begin to realise that rules of games are not arbitrary nor absolute but are convenient and sensible conventions that make playing easier and more enjoyable.

The seven-year-old is so filled with enthusiasm for life that we sometimes have to guard him against his own use of energy and prevent his becoming overtired. When he does go beyond his limits he spoils his work and becomes irritable and depressed. This swing from exuberance to depression can be seen often in most seven-year-olds. They can be so critical of their own work that they become miserable and may give up trying for a while. At other times, particularly at home, they complain that everyone is unfair, parents are unjust, brothers and sisters are a nuisance, no one cares about them. These moods pass quickly, especially if life in the home is busy and equable, and the seven-year-olds are back to their normal affectionate, joyous selves.

Most teachers say that they love to teach seven-year-olds because they are self-controlled, eager, spontaneous and confiding. They have a good command of language and can talk about their plans and exploits fluently and clearly. They still like adults and rely on them, but at this age their classmates are very important to them and the opinion of the group matters a great deal. Often at this age a child has a 'best friend' with whom he works, plays and shares secrets. This friend is usually of the same sex, but it is not uncommon to find a boy and a girl devoted to each other.

Eight to eleven

These are the years of stability and vitality. Emotionally the children are increasingly independent of the adults and membership of their own age group is more and more important to them. They are no longer so self-centred. They like to do things together and their groups stay together for longer and share more long-term projects than at any time before this. These are the years of vigorous activities like camping, swimming, hiking, roller-skating, complicated skipping and ball games, group games like cowboys and Indians, cops and robbers, and rounders. There is a good deal of wrestling and skirmishing of a friendly fashion — a more sophisticated form of the rough and tumble play of the nursery years. Children at this period are inventive, agile and graceful in their play.

Generally health is good and appetite sound in this period. The children eat well, use up the energy from their meals quickly and eat again. They tend to get tired suddenly after a long walk or an afternoon's hard play, and then they are irritable and edgy until sensible parents produce another meal.

Boys and girls mix well together except that from about the middle of this period some of the more masculine boys and the more feminine girls tend to make one-sex groups and ignore the others.

Conformity to group habits and standards is important. The children like to wear the same kind of clothes and to have the same kind of possessions as well as to do the same kind of things as the rest of their group. Children who do not or cannot conform are usually ignored or rejected and derided. This can be a major tragedy and often needs unobtrusive adult rescue tactics.

Children at this stage of development are content to let the adults run the framework of life, providing home, food, clothes, holidays, schooling and equipment like bicycles, books, and cameras. Within this framework they live their own lives, make their own decisions and choose their own friends. They recognise the authority of strong and effective adults but weak, vacillating and dishonest adults provoke their contempt and rejection. Too many weak adults in key positions at home or school lead to anxiety and confusion among the children.

They are willing to learn and enjoy working at school. They are deeply interested in finding out more about the things that interest them and the good teacher uses this as a point of contact. They resent a teacher who makes no effort to teach them although they are not aware of how much a good teacher does since he arranges it so that they appear to be doing most of the work. A poor teacher leaves them bored and slack, and this arouses rebellion and unsocial behaviour, but they respect and have true affection for a teacher who extends them and whom they can trust.

Occasionally groups of children at this age are infected suddenly by a kind of mob violence and then they seem to lose their usual control of passionate feelings. Authority has to step in firmly when this happens. A few children of this age are irresponsible and sometimes these are attractive to the others because they have certain qualities of leadership.

Throughout this junior school period the children are developing judgement and poise. One classroom assistant remarked in an observation exercise: 'I notice that when a nine-year-old is chosen to pick a team she always chooses her friends even if they are not good players but when a ten-year-old picks a team she chooses the best players.' By the time the child is ten-and-a-half he is a well-balanced person, alert, happy and stable, thoughtful and polite in the best sense — not because he has been taught to assume politeness but because he really feels pleasant towards other people. He is friendly and matter-of-fact with adults and cooperates in most ways with them. He enjoys life and is satisfied with home and school. Soon this stable period will be broken up by the onset of puberty and the long climb through adolescence but for most children this comes after they have left the junior school.

Further reading

Bowley, Agatha H., *The Natural Development of the Child*, 4th edn, Livingstone, 1957, particularly Chapters 1, 2 and 4.

Hadfield, J. A., *Childhood and Adolescence*, Penguin: Pelican, 1962, particularly Chapters 2, 3 and 4.

Hicks, Patricia, *Introduction to Child Development*, Longman, 1982.

Hutt, Corinne, *Males and Females*, Penguin Education, 1972.

Isaacs, Susan, *The Nursery Years*, 2nd edn, Routledge & Kegan Paul, 1932.

Lee, R. S., *Your Growing Child and Religion*, Penguin: Pelican, 1965, particularly Part 1.

Mussen, Paul H., *The Psychological Development of the Child*, Prentice-Hall, 1964.

New Scientist 61, No. 889ff. (1974). Sixteen weekly articles on developmental psychology, 14 March to 27 June.

Open University in association with Health Education Council, *The First Years of Life*, Ward Lock, 1979.

Sheridan, Mary D., *The Developmental Progress of Infants and Young Children*, HMSO Reports on Public Health and Medical Subjects, No. 102.

Tanner, J. M., *Education and Physical Growth*, University of London Press, 1961, particularly Chapters 1 and 2.

Refer also to the National Children's Bureau, 8 Wakley St, London EC1V 7QE for lists of publications.

Chapter 2

Play and learning I

The function of play

Play is the child's main business in life; through play he learns the skills to survive and finds some pattern in the confusing world into which he was born.

Through play he learns to control his body and develops balance and the coordination of brain, eyes and limbs; through play he explores the material world, collects facts and learns to think; through play he works out his emotional problems and learns to control his primitive feelings; through play he learns to be a social being and to take his place in his community.

These strands in his play are inextricably woven together, but we can sometimes see him solving problems on one front or another when we watch him. When he is awake and left to himself the young child spends most of his time playing. The urge to grow up and to control his environment is so strong that he gives all his energies to it and he learns more and at a greater rate in the first years of his life, before he goes to school, than at any other period of his life.

We are the adults responsible for him and we must give him the best conditions we can for his play. He needs space to play in which is safe and interesting, and he needs materials to play with. He needs long uninterrupted periods of time for his play and if we are sensible we arrange a daily routine for him which allows for this. The baby needs encouragement and approval, and he enjoys a grown-up playing with him. When he is a little older we can help him by a casual word of suggestion or by demonstrating a specific skill or showing him what to do at a critical moment. But mostly he likes to be left alone, with an encouraging adult in the background, to play in his own way until he is old enough to enjoy playing with other children.

Many people observing children have tried to separate different types of play. This is difficult because so many strands can be seen in almost any period of play. The child who seems only to be running, climbing or swinging for the sake of the physical satisfaction these movements give him, is at the same time consciously or unconsciously solving problems of speed and distance and spatial relationships. He may at the same time be pretending to be a lorry or a spaceman for all we know. However, for the sake of discussion we may try to look at some of the kinds of play we see most often with the children we know.

Vigorous physical play

Little children awake are rarely still. It is easier for them to move about than to sit or stand quietly. The baby spends the first eighteen months of his life when he is not asleep ceaselessly moving, learning to control the movements of his body. As his nervous system develops he manages more and more skilfully and is soon rolling over, sitting, reaching out, crawling, standing, walking, moving all the time. In the nursery school and the infant school we watch children becoming more and more agile. Watch any group of young children freely playing in a safe and well-equipped space and see them running, jumping, hopping, galloping, pushing, pulling, lifting, climbing trees and climbing-frames and ladders, hanging by their arms or their knees, swinging on swings, ropes and tyres, turning over bars, scrambling up nets, kicking and throwing balls, rolling down slopes, balancing on planks, riding tricycles, using rockers and roundabouts, digging, rolling tyres about, crawling through barrels, sliding, splashing, banging and hammering. Unless we fuss about taking care they are fearless.

In the junior school the children do all these things but more skilfully and powerfully. They ride bicycles instead of tricycles, they can swim and roller-skate, they throw and catch and kick and hit balls in organised ways, they wrestle and fight, they play leapfrog and somersault, and they delight in team games.

It is most important that we should give children a great deal of opportunity to use their bodies vigorously like this. They need to release energy and relax tension in these ways and of course they get an enormous amount of pleasure in the movement of their bodies — in the stretching and relaxing of opposite sets of muscles. Most of us can remember what pleasure there was in the stretched feeling of hanging by our arms and then letting go, or in running very fast across an open space.

Physical exercise is good for children because when they are active they breathe more deeply so that there is more oxygen carried about their bodies by the blood and they digest and absorb their food more thoroughly and throw off waste products more efficiently. Exercise is best if it is taken out-of-doors in fresh, moving air but in bad weather we can arrange for it indoors with windows open.

After exercise children sleep well and wake refreshed. Of course we must be careful not to let them overtire themselves, but left to themselves children tend to alternate periods of vigorous activity with periods of relaxation. Often when they have been running about outside for some time children come inside and sit quietly at a table working or go to an easel and paint or lie on the floor in the book corner. In the summer they fling themselves down under a tree and ask for a story, or go to water the rabbits in their enclosure, or lie face down in the grass watching ants among the stalks. Half an hour later we will see them on the climbing-frame or riding tricycles furiously round the paths.

Physical exercise is important for other reasons, too. Through it each child gets practice in the use of his body. He learns balance and control and gains agility. The coordination of eye, brain and muscles is steadily improved and with it comes self-confidence and a sense of achievement. These things are important to the child because they give him a feeling of being a valuable person in his community.

A child may enjoy vigorous movement for its own sake or as part of a game — he may be alone or with a group. For all we know, when we are watching him he is at the same time solving problems involved in judging distances and covering them at different speeds, in testing the amount of strength needed to pull a loaded wagon, in pushing a barrel up a slope, in lifting and stacking boxes, in turning a tricycle on a narrow path, in running and kicking a ball. The older a child becomes the more consciously and deliberately he works at such problems. To push and lift big material makes him feel powerful and he knows he is slowly gaining control over his world. For this reason vigorous physical play is especially good for aggressive and rebellious children who often prove to be leaders among their mates when their energies are directed into these channels. They show initiative and resource in making up ball games and taking the lead in a group organising plays about Batman and his enemies, cowboys and Indians, dances and musical games. We must remember that games such as cops and robbers and cowboys and Indians sometimes require one gang to lie or stand quite still for periods of several minutes, hiding or lying in wait, and this is a skilful thing for young children to do. The junior school child can do it more easily than the child in the infant school because his nervous system is more mature and allows him to have more control. The pre-school child finds it very difficult to lie absolutely still.

We are particularly fortunate in this country in having a mild and equable climate. There are very few days in any year when the children cannot go outside for some time at least and on the whole it is simple to arrange for them to play freely in and out of doors. In other countries when the indoor and outdoor temperatures may vary considerably it is not so easy.

When weather is bad and the children cannot go out we can with a little thought arrange for some vigorous play indoors. Infant schools have halls with physical education apparatus but corridors can be used as well and in the nursery school playrooms, bathrooms and corridors can be reorganised. Punch balls, rope ladders, knotted ropes and swings can be hung in doorways, trampolines can be put in safe places, boxes and planks can be arranged as adventurous walks, slides and nesting bridges are easily erected. Water play and easels can be moved into bathrooms and cloakrooms to make way for these things. Dancing and musical games can be given a special place on wet or foggy days and games like 'Simon says' or 'Follow my leader' can use up a great deal of energy.

Experimental play, exploration and discovery

To a certain extent it is true to say that all a young child's play has something experimental about it: he is always trying out new ways of doing familiar things and seeing what happens when he varies his materials and his methods. But some of his activities are more directly experimental than others.

The baby

For the child under two the whole of life is experimental. Before a baby crawls he is exploring his own body, his clothes, his pram, his cot, his simple playthings, his mother's face and breast. He uses his mouth, his eyes, ears, hands and body to collect facts about his surroundings. Here are some extracts from a mother's diary of her young baby which shows how early we can see this kind of activity:

> Yesterday a rattle was hung from the middle of the hood of the bassinet, R. (11 weeks) lying on her back. She looked at it. Later her hand by chance hit the rattle as she waved hand in air. Later was seen to be hitting the rattle repeatedly, first both hands moving but only hitting with left hand. Later right hand ceased to move and R. appeared to be hitting with left hand

deliberately and vigorously almost continuously for half an hour. She did not look at the rattle all the time, only at intervals. This was repeated this morning, hitting with the right hand, and this afternoon with both hands. Recently R. has been rubbing her face against her mother's and burrowing into it.

We have observed R. (16 weeks) look at her dangling rattle and then reach out to draw it towards her mouth.

At this age and for some months to come a baby uses his mouth to test things, feeling the different textures, hardness and softness, cold and warmth, sharp or rounded edges. But he soon begins to use his hands as well. Here is another extract from the diary:

R. (4½ months) tests fabrics and materials by feeling them intently, by stroking and passing her hand over them and scratching them. Today while sitting on mother's lap put out her hand and felt mother's face.

By the time she was sitting up this baby was experimenting more exactly:

R. (7½ months) has several rubber squeaking dolls. She has been observed to use within a few minutes three different ways of making each one squeak: (1) by squeezing it with her hand in the usual way, (2) by putting doll on floor and hitting it, (3) by holding doll by legs and banging it on floor.

Once the child can crawl the world expands and from then onwards he is constantly exploring his surroundings and experimenting, using his hands and body — pulling, pushing, tearing, opening, shutting, poking, filling, emptying, dragging, fitting together, tipping, dropping, picking up, banging, piling one thing on another. The ordinary furniture and fittings of the home are enough to keep him interested, together with a few simple playthings such as wooden spoons, tins, cartons, boxes, cotton reels, conkers, large beads, blocks, a ball, a rag doll, a few pieces of material and some things to play with in the bath. He follows his mother about the house copying her actions as she works. His parents keep the house safe for him by guarding fires and electric points and high windows and by keeping dangerous things out of his reach.

Although the young child does not appear to have a long attention span at this age but moves from one occupation to another fairly quickly, at times he is seen to do the same thing over and over again until he masters a way of handling the material or achieves the result he aims for. We often see children repeating the same actions for short periods over many days.

Having mastered the skill or discovered how something works he absorbs the result of his work and moves on to the next discovery. He is carrying on this kind of activity over a wide front so that he seems to be restlessly working all the time at a good many things.

Here is an account of a seventeen-month-old child working in this way.

> She became very much interested in a hanging switch for the light in the living room. It is of the push-through type. Pushing the button through one way puts on the light and pushing it back from the other side puts the light out. The first day she played with it she was able to push the button through from the side she held nearest her body but could not push it back. She appeared to grow furious with it and several times flung it angrily away from her, at other times more calmly handing it to her mother to be pushed back. The next day her mother observed her again playing with it. This time she pushed the button through, turned the switch round so that the button again faced her body and pushed it through again. This she repeated over and over again, and has continued to play in this way often since (several days).

During this second year of their lives children spend a good deal of time putting things in and out of other things, trying to fit things together and pushing things through holes. For instance they enjoy dropping cotton reels or conkers or blocks into empty cartons or boxes and tipping them out again. They like to play with a set of saucepans and lids, fitting each lid to the right saucepan by trial and error, and it is at this stage that they begin to play with posting boxes and hammer pegs.

Children do not always use the same material in the same way. Here are accounts of two children of about the same age using a posting box:

> R. (16 months) prefers to deal with all three objects of each shape before going on to another shape. Today her father reports seeing her put everything into its right hole although first trying a wrong hole for each object. He also reports that she was at one stage trying unsuccessfully to put a cube into its hole and asked for his help. He put it in for her. She tried the next cube and had difficulty and asked for his help. He said 'you have another go' and she tried again and got it in. Then she

put the third cube in. She then took off the lid, took out a cube, put on the lid, put cube through hole, took off lid, picked out a cube, put on lid, put cube through hole. Repeated three times.

E. (17 months) is not very keen on any toys except blocks that fit into each other and the posting box. She understands the principle of the posting box but rarely bothers to put all the objects in one by one. She puts in two or three, then lifts lid and dumps all the rest in.

During this time, too, the child is discovering and practising new ways of using his body — pulling himself up and walking, clambering over the furniture, climbing up and down stairs.

The pre-school child

By the time he is two years old the child needs more material to explore so we give him sand, clay, pastry, wood, tools, paint, wheels, pulleys, magnets, bolts and locks, scissors, paper, string, paste, fabrics, bricks, building materials of many kinds, things he can make different sounds with, and piles of clean junk. He has been playing with water from the time he was able to kick and splash in his bath but now he needs the opportunity to find out more about it.

There is not enough space to describe even some of the activities of children with all these materials but it is worth noting what they do with a few of the basic ones.

Sand   When we watch a group of children in a nursery school or playgroup playing with sand we usually see them doing some of these things: they let it run through their fingers, tip it from hand to hand, dig in it, eat it, cover their own and other children's feet and legs with it, stick grass, feathers, sticks and flowers into it, tip it in and out of tins, mix water with it and pack it into patty-tins and buckets to turn out as pies, watch it run out of holes in tins and colanders and strainers, smooth it out and draw on it with fingers or sticks, pile it into castles and buildings, fill bottles with it, using funnels and rubber tubes, shovel it into paper bags, trucks and boxes, carry it about in carts and trucks and wheelbarrows, weigh it, make roads and tracks for Dinky toys in it, use it as food or petrol in imaginative games.

The sand provided in nursery schools is of two kinds, silver sand which is fine and dry and easily runs through funnels and tubes, and coarser sand which packs and builds well when it is damp. Silver sand is often kept in a sandtray indoors and the coarser sand put into a sandpit outside. We can provide spades and spoons, patty-tins, buckets, funnels, tins, bottles, colanders and sieves for play with sand but the children think of many other things to use. At home, sand for indoor play can be kept in a basin or an old baby's bath.

Water   Home, playgroup and nursery school give children a great many opportunities to use water. They turn on taps and wash themselves, they flush lavatories, they bath dolls and wash dolls' clothes, they scrub furniture, they have tea parties and wash up, they arrange flowers in vases, they give water to pets and fill the bird-bath, they water the flowerbeds (and each other) with a hose and the potplants with a watering can, they tip water into the sandpit, they jump, splash and paddle in the pool, they make mud pies with water in the garden, they blow bubbles and beat up soapflakes, they 'paint' the walls, they use water in pistols, they sail boats. As well as all this they usually spend a good deal of time exploring the behaviour of water and things in it by play at the water-trolley or tub, or in the kitchen sink. Here they tip water from one tin to another, pour it through funnels, fill bottles, use strainers and tins with holes in sides and bottom, use rubber or plastic tubing in various ways, smack the surface to make waves, siphon the water into buckets, fish with lines and nets, experiment with floating and sinking objects and with materials that dissolve like salt or remain suspended like washing blue. At different times of year the children discover more facts about water. When it rains heavily some of the water that falls on the ground runs off in trickles and rivulets they can see and it rushes along in the gutters. But some of it seems to disappear into the earth. On hot sunny days water on the ground vanishes and the grass dries quickly. If they bring a bucket full of snow inside the snow is soon gone and the bucket has water in it. A saucer of water left outside in winter turns into ice and so does the water in the bird-bath. When they bring the saucer inside the ice turns into water and if they leave the saucer by the fire or put it on the radiator the water gradually disappears.

Bricks, blocks and building material   I shall use the words 'brick' and 'block' to mean the same thing. Americans and Australians usually use the word 'block' whereas the English more often say 'brick'.

If we watch we will see a definite development in the child's play with bricks. If we give him the opportunity the baby enjoys playing with bricks from an early age. By six months he is reaching out for a

small cube brick, grasping it with his whole hand and taking it to his
mouth. He can soon hold a small brick in each hand and will bang
them together. Six months later he enjoys putting small bricks into
cartons and boxes and tipping them out again. He likes to drop
bricks out of his pram or over the side of his playpen and when he is
a few weeks older be begins to pile bricks one on top of the other.
The two-year-old throws bricks about on the floor, fills boxes and
carts with them and then tips them all out again, puts them on the
floor in rows and pushes them along and builds towers with them
and knocks them down. Once he has the idea of building towers or
lines of bricks he experiments with variations of the same pattern.
For instance he will try putting big bricks on top of small ones or
alternating big and little bricks all the way up. Or he will put oblong
bricks along the floor alternately standing on their sides or their
ends. Soon he is building several towers side by side to make a fence
and putting several rows on the floor close together to make a
platform.

We can often watch children reasoning and working out problems
of spatial relationships with bricks. For instance trying to make a
bridge or a roof seems to occupy many two-year-olds for long
periods during their play with bricks and blocks. Mothers, teachers
and assistants report seeing two- and three-year-olds trying to fit a
long block across two piles of cubes or two long bricks standing on
end. When they find the distance between the side posts is too great
for another long brick to span it they try several ways of placing the
bridge brick. Some teachers report children sitting thoughtfully in
front of their bricks for some minutes as if working out the problem,
and then trying new ways of placing the bricks. Once they have
solved the problem of spanning spaces between blocks the children
go on to build more and more elaborate structures.

Four-year-olds make complicated buildings with blocks and call
them houses, garages, castles, prisons, wharves, railway stations and
airports. They like to use other playthings such as Dinky toys, boxes
and pieces of wood, little figures, tractors and cars, ships and aeroplanes along with their bricks.

Nursery schools provide large numbers of bricks in all shapes and
sizes. Many nurseries like having large sets of unit blocks where the
smaller blocks are exact fractions of the larger ones. There can also
be blocks in the shape of cylinders, arches, laths, pyramids and
cones. Some large hollow blocks are also useful for big, quick
building.

Building play outside with bigger material is an extension of play
with blocks. Usually a group of the older nursery children work

together on this. Wooden boxes and planks and barrels are piled into buildings onto and into which the children climb and crawl, working out dramatic games. Sometimes the building is made round a centre which may be the climbing-frame or a tree. Branches, logs, tyres and large cartons may be incorporated; a blanket or a tarpaulin may be used to drape over part of the pile. Single lines of boxes often appear in play of this kind but there is great variation both in the shape of the building and in the material used.

The child at school

Modern primary and infant schools give children the same basic materials to experiment with as the nursery school gives to the pre-school child.

The five-year-old does many of the same things with sand as the younger child does. If he has not had the opportunity to play freely with sand before he comes to school he may play with it in these ways for a considerable length of time. But gradually his use of sand becomes more organised. We can see six- and seven-year-olds making race tracks and roads and harbours in the sandpit, working in groups and using their model cars and ships in sophisticated ways, planning, measuring and reasoning together. Sand is a useful material for exact weighing and for finding out about volume and capacity, and teachers provide opportunities and tools (such as spoons, cups and measures) for it to be used in these ways.

Water play becomes more precise, too. Children can use exact measures with water — litre and 500 ml measures, for instance. They can weigh it and learn first to weigh the vessel it is carried in. They use it to dissolve a variety of substances and discover that there are many substances it won't dissolve. They use it in carefully adjusted amounts in bottles to get a scale of musical sounds. They boil it and find out about steam and condensation.

By play with balloons, inner tubes, football bladders and beach balls they find they can use air in different ways, put it to work and weigh it. They continue to play with building and constructing material a great deal, becoming more and more skilful in planning and carrying out their projects.

Their investigations into the environment widen in scope. When they can read and write they can follow suggestions and instructions from books and work cards and carry out organised experiments, recording results. As time goes on in the primary school the children's manipulation of material leads them to collect and record information about such things as air and water pressure, levers, machines, momentum, magnetism, electricity, heat, evaporation, mapping and surveying, how plants and animals live and grow and the conditions they need to be healthy.

The children are given books, maps, diagrams and models to help them in their own investigations, and the modern school also uses radio, television, films, video-tapes, computers and all the other technical equipment available to enlarge the scope of the children's work and to consolidate their discoveries. Each child is able to link up his results with those of his mates and to exchange ideas with them because he is encouraged from the beginning to discuss his work freely. They can then plan new investigations based on their combined discoveries.

Learning from experimental play

It is not difficult for us to see what children in the infant and junior schools are learning when we see them working busily with rulers and tape measures, weighing sand or flour, watering class pets, recording the growth of bean shoots or cutting and folding shapes of coloured paper. It is not always so easy to understand what the baby or the nursery school child is learning when he is playing. But the baby and the toddler are laying the foundation for all the learning they will do later in school by gathering information, solving problems and finding patterns in what lies about them.

The young child investigates problems bodily. He literally crawls about them and through them probing with his senses and using all his body to collect information. The facts he collects are stored in his mind so that without having to think about it he calls each one up later on when the time comes to use it and build on it. By the time he goes to school he has accumulated a great deal of information by his own efforts and by listening to and talking with grown-ups and other children.

By his play with all sorts of things the baby gradually finds out a great deal about the *properties of various materials* — hardness, softness, coldness, warmness, smoothness, furriness, scratchiness, sharpness, roundness; some things can be bent, some can be squeezed, some can be sucked up, others have to be chewed; some things have a strong smell, some are bright to look at.

He finds out that *things behave differently*: water and sand both spill out of a cup but sand in a tray will stay pushed up in a pile at one end and water will not do this. Water wets things. Some things make a noise when they are dropped, other things bounce and make very little sound, other things again break into pieces. Some materials tear easily but other things that look much the same don't tear but can be used for wrapping up dolls, or putting over his own head, or wiping up water from the floor. Some parts of the furniture slide in and out, other parts open and shut. Some pieces of furniture can be pushed about, others stand very firmly. Some toys move easily when he pulls them, others have to be pushed hard before they will move. His ball rolls down a slope but his teddy bear slides down. A drum or a tin can will slide in one position (flat or on its base) and roll in another (on its side). He can roll down a slope himself if he alters his shape to be more like the ball or the tin. If he puts out his arms and becomes more the shape of the teddy bear he slides instead of rolling.

The baby smiles at his mother and other people some time before he truly separates his mother out from the others; his wariness with strangers, which begins at six to seven months, marks the beginning of his being able to *separate out one from many* and after that he slowly becomes more competent to do this with people and play material.

The little child early has experience of *two similar things* — his own two hands, two arms put into two coat sleeves, two legs, two leg-holes in his pants (mother says 'now the other one'), two feet, two socks, two shoes, two eyes. A mother gives this record of her daughter one year and eight months old:

> She asked me to take off her shoes by presenting one shoe and saying 'off' and then the other saying 'two off'. Later, looking in the mirror with me she pointed to one of her ears and said 'ear' and then to the other and said 'two ear'. Next day she said 'shoe' and then 'two shoe' to her shoes.

There is not enough evidence for us to say that this little girl had the concept of two, or understood twoness, but we can say that she recognised two things as being similar and could separate one from the other. Little children can soon learn to recite the names of the numbers but it is usually several years more before they learn actually to count objects, that is, to point to each of a row of objects as they name its number in the row.

As they play freely with all sorts of material children become aware of *relative size and weight* (big, little, bigger than, smaller than, heavier than). The little girl mentioned above was, at one year and ten and a half months, carrying two dolls upstairs, one large and the other tiny. She said 'Baba 'eavy'. Her mother said 'Which one is heavy?' and the child showed her the large doll.

Relative quantity (more than, less than, fewer than) and *capacity* (how much will it hold?), the different *shapes* of things, *space*, *distance* and *area* are all practical experiences for the little child as he plays. He is concerned a good deal with *spatial relationships*. For instance, he learns the dimensions of the carpet as he discovers he can crawl over it; he begins to understand phrases like 'beside the chair' or 'behind the sofa' or 'sitting between Mummy and Daddy'; he walks around in Daddy's shoes which are much too big for his feet; he climbs from one rung to another on the climbing frame; sometimes he scribbles over the curved surface of his ball instead of on a flat piece of paper; he rolls his plasticine into a long worm and then coils it into a plate or into a curved cup; he takes a cardboard box and opens it out flat or squashes it into a different shape; he curls a piece of card into a cylinder or folds it into a little basket; he squeezes his balloon and the painted face on it bulges out in one place and looks big while the rest of it stays small; he notices that when he is making shadows by holding things in front of the light the shadows look different when they fall on the curved furniture from the way they look on the wall.

Children are interested in *speed*, too, and are a good deal concerned about it when they are just learning to walk because other children run about close to them and knock them over. The different rates at which their balls roll or their carts pull along or their tops spin interest them, but by the time they go to school they are still not clearly aware of how fast things like cars and lorries, the control of which is still outside their experience, are travelling along roads. This is one reason why we must watch them so carefully on the streets.

Of course the idea of *time* is connected with the idea of speed because of covering a given length of ground in a space of time. The concept of time is particularly puzzling to the little child: 'Is it morning time?' 'Am I a big girl now?' 'Is today tomorrow? You said we'd see Granny tomorrow.' 'Where do the days go to?' Sometimes it seems a very long time to wait half a day for a promised treat, at other times the morning's play seems to be over in a flash.

Direction is another idea the child becomes familiar with — 'over there', 'come here', 'Where's Johnny?', the wind blowing from one side, right and left hands, spoons and forks set on the dinner table, upwards and downwards. He has to turn his head from side to side or tip it up and down to watch things happening.

He becomes familiar with *force* when he pushes his wheel-barrow, digs with his spade in the sand and the earth, turns the door-handle, saws a piece of wood or hammers nails. He experiences *balance and equilibrium* when he builds towers with his bricks, puts a plank on top of his pile of boxes, sits on a fence or a rail, or plays on the seesaw and the rocking horse.

He experiences something about *proportion* when he uses his face flannel which has red and white stripes, when he throws mother's cushion about and sees that it is blue on one side and green on the other, when he hears his big brother say 'half these sweets are pink and half of them are white', when he plays with blocks on which each face is of different texture or a ball with segments of different patterns or when he wears a twotoned pullover.

He first learns about *series* of things by climbing steps and stairs, by running a stick along a paling fence, by setting his bricks out in repeating patterns, by threading beads on a string, or standing up a row of cotton reels or skittles or by playing with a set of Russian dolls or nesting cubes.

Young children have little idea of *cause and effect* in the material world because they have not enough experience and not enough knowledge to work on. To them the world must appear to be managed in a magical or an arbitrary way. But little by little, as they see more and more of the pattern of behaviour in the world through their experimental play, they begin to see something of what makes things work. The baby learns that his mother comes when he cries but he has to repeat the experience a great many times before he can rely on it. The little child must turn on the tap over and over again before he is sure that water will come out every time and not only when the sun shines or when the window is closed or when Mummy is wearing an apron. Bit by bit, by doing and by watching and later by asking questions he pieces together the puzzle. Children have by no means collected all the information they need to understand cause and effect by the time they go to school and that is why the good school still gives them opportunities to explore and experiment with many different materials under a variety of conditions.

These are only some of the things that babies and little children learn by playing freely and experimenting with all kinds of material. If we watch them and use our imagination to try to see the world as they see it, without the adult conceptions we take for granted, we shall realise how many more things than these they are learning and how it would be impossible for them to learn what we expect them to learn at school without this basis of information they themselves have amassed. A child has to experience a thing before he can understand it or believe in it: so that although we may try to teach him mathematics and the sciences and to reason and think for himself to solve problems, unless he has had time and opportunity to *experience* fundamental concepts he will not have the tools to work with and much of what we try to teach him will never have any real meaning for him.

In order fully to use his experiences for learning, thinking and reasoning the little child needs language so we should talk freely with him about what he is doing. This clothes his play with words.

Further reading

Chesters, Gwendolen E., *The Mothering of Young Children*, 2nd edn, Faber, 1956, particularly Chapters 4, 5 and 6.

Gardner, D. E. M., *The Education of Young Children*, Methuen, 1956, particularly Chapters 2 and 3.

Hegeler, Sten, *Choosing Toys for Children*, Tavistock, 1963.

Hutt, C., *Exploration and Play in Children*, Symposia of the Zoological Society of London, 1966, 18, 61–81.

Matterson, E. M., *Play with a Purpose for the Under-Sevens*, Penguin, 1965.

May, D. E., *Suggestions for Play Activities for Young Children*, Save the Children Fund, 1967.

Page, H., *About Buying Toys*, Consumer Council, 1965.

Page, H., *Children Learning Through Scientific Interests*, National Froebel Foundation, 1966.

Roberts, Vera, *Playing, Learning and Living*, A. & C. Black Ltd, London, 1971.

Sheridan, Mary, *Spontaneous Play in Early Childhood*, National Foundation for Educational Research, 1977.

Chapter 3

Play and learning II

Creative play

There is no clear line between experimental and creative play: the one merges into the other imperceptibly. Children love making things, but the first step is always finding out about the materials and how to use them. Then the child who experiments with a new material or medium often finds he has made something new and exciting.

The child who, left to himself, writes a poem, or directs a play, or makes up a dance or performs a mime is creating something, but for the sake of the immediate discussion we will use the words 'creative play' to cover only drawing, painting, modelling and making things. In this kind of play children explore the behaviour and properties of the materials we give them with all their senses. They feel the hardness or softness of pencils and chalks, they watch paint run, drip and splash, they experience with their muscles how paint flows on to paper and from a brush and how finger paint oozes over the surface they are pressing on and how clay responds to thumping and nails to hammering. They experience the feel of wet clay and paint drying on their skin, we know they notice the smells of clay and plasticine and paint because they comment on them. One four-year-old boy constantly avoided the brown paint put out for him because 'it smells loud'. They lick pencils, paint brushes, crayons, chalk and clay and they talk about the noises they hear their saws and hammers making.

Drawing and painting

If we watch our children drawing and painting and look at their work we will see that the youngest ones, up to about three years old, are mostly trying out tools and experimenting in how to use materials. From then on, through the nursery school and infant school and into the first years of the junior school the children are drawing and painting in a simple, logical way, using forms and shapes (for instance, to represent people, animals, houses, cars, aeroplanes) which are not like the ones adults use but which are very much the same as those which children all over the world use. In fact children have a drawing language of their own. Towards the middle of the junior school years we notice that they begin to abandon this language and try more and more to draw like adults. By the time they leave the junior school most children seem to be seeing things and trying to represent them like grown-ups do. Many of them become dissatisfied with their efforts and give up drawing and painting seriously unless the teaching in their secondary school is encouraging and stimulating.

If we let children alone to explore the materials and tools they will make what they want to. Their expression will mature naturally as time goes on if we do not try to impose our ideas on them. We can impose our standards as much by implication (by our tone of voice, by not sparing their work much of our attention or by praising skill of execution rather than creative and original ideas) as by direct criticism or suggestion and we have to watch this in ourselves because if we impose on them our standards before they are ready to adopt them we damage their natural development.

Babies begin to scribble as soon as they can hold a pencil firmly and from then onwards for many years scribbling and drawing is a favourite occupation.

In nursery groups and in the infant school we should make sure that the children have every opportunity we can give them for drawing. There should always be set out paper of various kinds and pencils of differing hardness (H, HB, B, 2B, 4B) and differing thickness. Coloured pencils, chalks, large crayons, charcoal, felt and fibre tipped pens and ballpoint pens should also be readily available.

Drawing goes on and on through the years of childhood. It is more convenient than painting because it can be done at any time in any place where there is a scrap of paper and a pencil, in school, at home, in the garden, in bed, in trains and cars and aeroplanes, on railway stations and at bus stops, in church, in shops or at the hairdresser while Mother is busy.

Young children see the world with clear, fresh eyes and put a great deal of detail into their drawings. Drawing often merges with fantasy and make-believe, the children telling long involved stories as they draw. I knew a group of children between seven and nine years who over a long period used toilet rolls to draw the continuing adventures of their imagined characters, in endless strip pictures. They would draw, murmuring to themselves and exchanging episodes and incidents with each other for hours at a time, especially during school holidays and at weekends.

Children sometimes draw more freely at home than at school after they enter the junior school if the atmosphere in school is not encouraging. They are quick to sense disparagement of their free drawing efforts and tend then to draw only in 'art' lessons. On the other hand ridicule or criticism at home will drive their efforts underground and if the school atmosphere is also unsympathetic they may give up altogether. 'Art' then becomes just another 'subject'. Fortunately most junior schools today give constant opportunities and encouragement for drawing freely.

Painting needs a little more preparation than drawing but gives endless opportunities for delight and growth. Children are usually ready to be introduced to painting at about two years old and from that age onwards wherever there are groups of children in our care we want to give them opportunity and time to paint.

We need to provide quantities of paper of different colour, thickness and texture — kitchen paper, lining paper, wallpaper, newspaper, sugar paper, wrapping paper. Where money is short, effort and initiative will provide paper from many unlikely sources. Children do not mind painting on printed newspaper of fair quality if there is no other paper. The one thing they seem to dislike is to use the back of someone else's painting. The sheets of paper should be large — about 50 by 45 cm — to give plenty of room for big arm movements in the younger children and generous scope for the ideas of the older ones. Junior school children may want to cut down the size of the paper for some work. The paper need not always be rectangular; some teachers like to tear or cut paper in irregular shapes. This is certainly useful if scrap paper has to be used from time to time. Much bigger sheets are needed for group work.

The paint used with young children is usually powder paint bought in bulk, although poster paints are sometimes used and cold water dyes are popular in some schools. Powder paints are usually mixed by the adults for the youngest children and a little of each colour put into half-pound jam-jars. The older children like to mix their own and may be given a teaspoonful of powder in each of a set of bun tins. A few drops of liquid detergent makes the powder easier to mix and wastes less, or hot instead of cold water may be used.

Some teachers believe that the primary colours only, together with white and black, should be given, others believe that as many colours as possible should be given to the children. In any case it is a good idea to give even the youngest children some opportunity to mix their colours. As soon as he begins to paint a child will notice how colours run into each other and make new colours on his paper and this interests him. The two- and three-year-olds may be content to mix their colours only on the paper but even at this stage some of them like to have an enamel plate to mix colours on.

Jam-pots of paint should be put where they will not easily be knocked over because this is discouraging as well as being wasteful. Some easels have troughs to hold the jars, or they can be put into a cake tin standing on a chair nearby.

Brushes should be large for the smaller children but a variety of sizes should be available for experiment. As the finer muscles of hand and eye mature children like to use finer brushes for more detailed work. We usually give the youngest children round hog-bristle brushes size 10 or 12 and put one brush into each jar of paint. There is no reason why they should not also have a few flat hog-brushes to try. But any brush, or a piece of sponge or even a kitchen dish-mop is better than nothing if the child at home wants to paint. The older children learn to use one brush and wash it before using a fresh colour. They need a large jar of water for this. Most children enjoy washing paintbrushes, shaking them and storing them, handle downwards, in a jar at the end of a day's work.

There is no particular position in which children should paint. Easels are convenient because they take up little room and they encourage sweeping arm movements. But children paint very well on the floor or on tables and paint does not run so much on a flat surface. We protect the clothes of the young children by giving them aprons. An old shirt with the sleeves cut short and worn back to front makes a good overall.

Opportunity to use charcoal, crayons and chalks together with paint should be given to the children. They will discover all kinds of new procedures and exciting effects. A box in which are put milk-bottle tops (washed and boiled), feathers, scraps of material and coloured papers of different kinds, may be kept near the painting area in the playroom or classroom. Nursery school children some-times like to make pictures by gumming these on to their paintings. The children in the infant school use collage material a good deal, especially for large pictures designed and made by them in groups. These sometimes illustrate a story they have enjoyed or celebrate a special occasion — Christmas, Bonfire Night, a local festivity — and are sometimes about an imaginative theme of their own.

Fingerpainting

This is a different form of activity from painting with a brush and is particularly popular with the younger children from two to six years. It consists of smoothing handfuls of thick paste over a flat surface and then making patterns in it with hands and fingers or a comb. The enjoyment for the children comes from feeling they are making and from having a messy form of play approved by the adults. The paste may be made in several ways or commercially prepared paste products may be used. Some teachers find that the smoothest base and the one which carries colours best is a home-made paste of plain flour, soap flakes and talcum powder mixed well together and then mixed with water. Colour may be added during the making so the child is given small basins of coloured paste from which he takes handfuls, or he may be given a basin of colourless paste and a number of little fish-paste pots each with a little dry powder colour in it. He spreads his paste and then from time to time sprinkles a little dry colour on to it from his pots, or a few drops of food colouring make a change.

The surface on which the paste is spread may be a large piece of paper made damp with a sponge, an enamel tray or just the laminated plastic top of a table. The child's sleeves are rolled up and his clothes are covered with a large apron. If he wants to take a 'picture' from the pattern he has made he can put a piece of paper down on it, smooth it over lightly and lift it off. He then has an offset.

Designs and patterns

Making designs and patterns can be fun and can be done very simply even by the nursery school child whose spontaneous paintings sometimes themselves show a repetitive pattern. More skilful and complicated patterns can be made as he grows older. Making patterns is a more organised activity than painting pictures and usually needs more direct help from adults, at least to begin with. Most teachers can suggest various ways of making designs and patterns. Among these are string patterns (made by soaking soft string in paint, dropping it in a loose pattern on to a flat surface and taking an offset. There are a number of variations of this method); 'kitchen' patterns (made by dripping trails of clear paste on a large sheet of paper and then sprinkling dry rice, tea, coffee, breakfast cereals, lentils, salt, split peas and other similar materials on to the paste; these patterns often smell delicious and are known in one nursery school at least as 'smellies'); potato and stick printing patterns; tie-dyeing patterns; and rubbings of different kinds.

Modelling

Three materials are most often used for modelling, which is another way of making interesting shapes and designs. They are dough, clay and plasticine. Modelling is valuable, apart from the delight of creating for its own sake, because the child is working in three dimensions so he is making shapes and patterns in the round instead of flat. He is also expressing the feelings he has in his fingers, hands, arms and body and not only those he has in his mind and eyes.

Dough   Dough is a favourite play material with pre-school and young infant school children. Most of its popularity probably comes from the fact that Mother makes pastry and cooks it for the family to eat. Dough to be rolled out and cut with pastry cutters by the children, cooked and eaten can be made of plain flour and water with a little salt added. It should be made fresh every day. However, if more salt is added so that the mixture is half flour and half salt the dough can be used to make models of cakes and tarts and lollies: these can be baked in a slow oven until they are hard and then painted and varnished and used in the wendy house or the shop. They will last for weeks. A simple dough for modelling at home can be made from flour, salt and water with a few drops of cooking oil added. It can be coloured with food colouring or powder paint. This dough will keep for several days if it is put into a plastic box in a cold place between periods of use. A dough which keeps for a long time is made by mixing one cup of cornflour with two cups of bicarbonate of soda and half a pint of water in a saucepan and stirring over a moderate heat until the mixture looks like mashed potato. Cool it and knead till smooth. Wrap in film and keep airtight until needed. Objects modelled in this dough dry hard slowly and may be painted or varnished.

Children like the soft feel of dough, its stretchiness and its homely smell. They usually enjoy clearing up after dough play because it takes some time to clean off the rollers and boards and cutters and this means using water and perhaps a scraper. Children using dough are usually quiet and contented, talking peacefully together and not being as energetic or fiercely concentrated as they often are with clay.

Clay   Clay can be bought in bulk fairly cheaply in powder form so that most nursery schools, playgroups and primary schools can have enough always ready for each child to work with. Teachers know it is messy so they make provision for this because its value to the children outweighs its mess. To the children its messiness is one of its joys. An easily cleaned table surface, a sheet of plastic or sheets of newspaper to protect the floor and work aprons to protect the children's clothes are all that are necessary to keep the mess within bounds. Stray bits of dried clay are easily swept up at clearing-up time.

Apart from the messiness which pleases the youngest children and the satisfying feel of working with it that all children experience, clay is also a useful play material because by pounding, banging, squeezing and kneading it the frustrated or resentful child can find relief. It is a simple and direct way to smash or destroy something, if that is how he feels, without doing any harm. He can then very easily restore what he has destroyed by building the clay up again.

Young children roll the clay into long 'snakes' or pat and scoop it into different shapes. They later find they can make shapes like animals and people by pushing and pulling it. They discover that if they pull bits of it out too much they break off and are hard to put on again. But on the whole the nursery school child just enjoys working the clay. Older children, from six or seven onwards, usually have some idea of what they want to model and plan their work, often using tools as well as their hands.

If the young child makes something he likes out of clay he can let it dry slowly and then paint it. Some teachers mix colour with the clay, others prefer to leave it the natural colour. Some others again do not approve of clay being painted or coloured at all but show the children how to polish the dried work by dry rubbing or by using wax. The work of older children may be fired and glazed if the school has a kiln.

A few children are reluctant to play with clay at first because it is 'dirty'. No one urges them to use it but after painting and playing with dough for some weeks or months they usually pick out a lump of fairly dry clay and begin to push it about. After that they gradually become more adventurous with it.

Plasticine   Some years ago it was fashionable to banish plasticine from nursery and infant schools on the grounds that it was not as good for the children to work with as clay. But as it is *not* clay, and to have plasticine as well does not prevent the children using clay, the argument lost force. Most teachers want the children to have as many different experiences as possible. Plasticine feels and smells different from clay. It can be pounded and kneaded if the child has a big enough lump but most children like to take enough to make a ball between their hands and roll it out into a worm and press it back again into a ball and squeeze it in one hand. It rolls into finer strips than clay. Arms and legs of people and animals and handles of cups and jugs stick on better than with clay and the children use it in houseplay and make-believe play much more than they use clay.

One great advantage of plasticine is its adaptability in holding and sticking other materials together, and in providing extra characters or missing parts in different kinds of play activities. For instance one can quickly make for the dolls' house a family who can sit or kneel or stand in any position; or a driver for the Dinky tractor; or animals for the zoo. It makes a firm base on which to hold up candles, or flags, or signals, or twigs for trees; it holds together a train of match-boxes; it will make a dolls' house birthday cake or the missing lid for a doll's teapot; it makes splendid fences for farms or bollards in traffic games with small cars; it makes gloves and shoes for dolls; one can mend a broken animal or aeroplane with it until more permanent repairs can be made. Then it can very easily be removed and rolled up again and put away.

Some teachers object to the dreary colour plasticine soon becomes when the children mix all the colours together but the children don't seem to mind this and many schools only order one colour. In cold weather when it is hard the plasticine can be softened by being kneaded in small pieces with a little Vaseline on the hands.

On the whole it is the older nursery children and the primary school children who make the most use of plasticine and they show surprising ingenuity with it.

Sand and mud

Everybody who has made a castle on the beach knows what good creative material damp sand is. The youngest children in the nursery school and play group who are mostly experimenting with sand to see how it behaves and what it feels like discover that it makes interesting shapes when they tip it out of buckets and tins. The older nursery school children are familiar with sand as a modelling material and use it for complicated building operations. Four-year-olds make houses and castles by putting several bucketfuls of sand together in patterns. They sometimes use pieces of wood or blocks to get high levels by putting a second storey of sand pies on blocks between the first set or on wood across them. Making gardens is another favourite game with four-year-olds in the sandpit, and shells, twigs, feathers, buttons, paper, leaves and pebbles are used in patterns to set them out. The children sometimes decorate their sand-houses with these things, too. They also use the sand to draw on by smoothing it over with their hands or a piece of wood and then 'writing' or drawing patterns on it with fingers or twigs.

Children in the infant school use sand in similar decorative ways and are skilful in trickling it in patterns on the ground. The complicated building they do with sand for their imaginative games is also, of course, creative activity as well.

Children lucky enough to be allowed to play with mud find that whole streets and towns can be laid out and will dry without crumbling, lasting several days unless there is rain. If the soil is mainly clay the children find they can wash out loam and stones and use the clay for modelling. There is a particular satisfaction in digging out your own clay and making something with it. Junior school children can pan the clay and refine it and then fire their pots if the school has the equipment. The feel of working with mud is quite different from the feel of sand and children who discover this enjoy squeezing it through their fingers and smoothing it over and over.

Bricks and blocks

Some teachers believe that children use bricks and blocks as creative material much as they use paint and clay. Certainly the designs of their towers and buildings and the way in which they use differently shaped and coloured blocks to make repeating patterns supports this view. Once children are confident in their handling of blocks their imagination and creative impulses can have free play and they show great variety and flexibility in their use of the material where the school or playgroup has a large enough supply of bricks and blocks to encourage original work.

Wood

Every parent knows how attractive Dad's tools are to his young children and the woodwork bench is one of the most popular centres of activity in any nursery school and primary school. Playgroups who have limited space for storage sometimes find it difficult to have a bench but some have solved the problem by finding a large, stout wooden box or packing case (unfortunately these are scarce now) which can be used as a bench by day, placed on its side so that a clamp or vice can be screwed on. At night it acts as a storage place for other play materials. Failing a packing case a strong, low table can be used. Inside corners of box or table can be strengthened with angle iron or corner brackets.

For the youngest children in the nursery school hammering is the main attraction of the woodwork corner and it is a good idea to have a few small logs of wood which are to be used for hammering in nails. This avoids having the bench itself used for this. The children willingly accept the rule that we don't hammer nails into the bench if they have plenty of opportunity to hammer them in somewhere else. They quickly grow through this stage and then they want to know how to use the other tools.

We should give the children real tools, sets of toy tools are not strong enough. We should provide clamps and a vice, if we can afford it, several kinds and weights of hammer (including a claw hammer), pincers, saws (a small metal hacksaw, known to chain stores and school suppliers as a junior hacksaw, is best for the nursery school), rulers, carpenters' pencils, bradawls, gimlets, screwdrivers, several files and a rasp. In the infant school a hand drill and a tenon saw can be added and in the junior school it is usually possible to add several more advanced tools such as a brace and bit, hand saws and a plane. Arrangements should be made to keep these tools in an orderly manner, hanging by the bench, and the children will soon take it for granted that they put tools away after using them. Playgroup leaders can make a set of wall pockets which can be rolled up after use each day. From the nursery upwards there should be sandpaper, glue, primer and paint available close to the woodwork bench and we should have plenty of nails and screws in boxes. The children should be shown how to hold and use the tools and then left alone although advice on certain techniques such as differences in the use of nails and screws, and how to place wood to hold wheels (avoiding end grain, for instance) and to put on the wheels themselves will be necessary from time to time. As using tools is one of the operations where adult help and advice is especially necessary to avoid accidents and frustration, grown-ups must tread a careful path between too much oversight and too much freedom.

We should have a large supply of wood of various kinds and thicknesses always on hand. Woodyards and undertakers are usually helpful in giving away bags of scrap wood. Wood is a beautiful material. Many sensitive children love to feel it and smell it and look at it and just carry it about. It is interesting to discover what possibilities children see in pieces of wood. A father recently brought to an infant school a sackful of 6 mm reddish wood 10 cm wide cut into lengths of about 45 cm. A few pieces were triangular. Two boys of five years seized immediately upon this and worked for over an hour, finally bringing to listen to the morning story four 'men' 90 cm high made with triangular heads, and bodies, arms and legs made of the wood pieces simply but strongly nailed together. These 'men' were affectionately accepted by the other children and included in all the class activities until the end of term.

Waste material

Most day nurseries, nursery schools and primary schools today keep a junk box, and most playgroups do too if they have enough space to make it possible. Into this box is put from day to day clean waste material which members of staff collect and parents bring or send and which is used by the children to make things. Children between nine months and three years like to explore and handle the material but from about three years onwards they begin to use it to build and make all sorts of things — houses, people, animals, ships, trains, lorries, cars, witches, giants, creatures from outer space, lighthouses, windmills, or just 'things'.

Waste material put into the junk box includes cardboard, matchboxes, tubes from kitchen paper and toilet rolls, cotton reels, eggboxes, scraps of material, ribbon, tape, bottle tops, corks, plastic containers, bottles, tins, cartons, buttons, wool, rubber tubing, feathers, pebbles, beads, nuts, shells, conkers, bits of dowel, wire, flex, rubber bands, paper fasteners, paper clips and string. Together with this material we put within easy reach scissors, wire cutters, paste, glue, plasticine, paint, brushes, pencils and felt-tipped pens.

Working alone, as the nursery child does, or in groups as the older infant school children begin to do, the children produce work with these materials which is truly creative. It is the adaptability of the material which seems to appeal to the children who love to explore its infinite possibilities. Handling and turning it over gives them pleasure and stimulates their creative imagination. We are often amazed at the length of time and the amount of concentration they spend on this activity.

Some very beautiful three-dimensional pictures and sculptures and abstract designs have been made in junior schools from waste material. Junior school children also use it freely in carrying out projects connected with their other work as well as in purely 'creative' ways.

The value of creative play

To sum up, it is most important that we should give children the opportunity for creative play. Some of the reasons for this are:

1. Exploration of different materials is the first step to making something and the pleasure of manipulation is valuable in itself. Children should be able to feel, smell, see and even taste and listen to the materials they are going to use. A three-year-old boy said of the sand he was pushing firmly together to make turrets on his castle: 'It creaks when I squeeze.' He held every scoopful of sand close to his ear as he shaped it between his hands.
2. The joy in achievement every time a child makes something which

satisfies him consolidates his confidence in himself and his belief in the stability of his world.

3. By making things and painting pictures children show us what is in their minds without having to use words. We can see what is important to them because they make or paint this more often than other things and usually larger or in more detail. An amusing example of this was reported by a mother who described the picture her four-year-old son painted of his baby brother's christening party. His father appeared as a figure of medium size in gala dress; his mother was an insignificant figure in the background; the baby was a tiny spot of paint in a kind of box down in one corner of the paper; the centre of the paper was taken up by a giant painting of the boy himself standing beside a large cake whose every decoration was given in detail.

    Sometimes an anxious or troubled child gives us a clue about what is worrying him in his painting or his modelling or building.

4. Children often have passionate feelings of fury and frustration towards other children and adults. Instead of showing these by shouting, hitting, kicking or throwing things about the children can find relief by banging and pounding clay, smashing it up and rolling it out; or by hammering nails into wood; or by digging furiously in the sandpit; or by brushing great swathes of colour across paper. Gradually the intensity of feeling drains away and the occupation itself becomes interesting. The lonely, anxious or timid child finds solace and delight in creative play.

5. One of the most valuable aspects of creative play is what we might call its quality of restitution. Children constantly feel helpless and clumsy in the face of adult power and ability. They feel guilty about their frequent feelings of hostility towards adults whom they admire and love and find it hard to believe that they themselves are lovable and of value to the adults when so often they seem only to be able to break things and be dirty and troublesome. By giving children opportunities to be creative we show them that they can be clever and constructive and can contribute to their world something that is valued by the grown-ups. We also show them that good things can come out of destruction. They learn what every artist learns, that something must be destroyed so that something new can be created. White paper is attacked with paint; a lump of clay must be broken and smashed to be built up again; coloured paper is cut with scissors to make beautiful patterns; wood is sawn into bits to make an aeroplane. This practical lesson, that creation can come out of destruction, gradually builds up confidence and assurance in the child.

The fact that much of the material we give them is messy also reassures children. They do not mind being messy, often they can't help it; their ineptitude and clumsiness makes them untidy and causes them to spill things; their interest in finding out about everything results in dirty clothes and hands. But adults dislike mess so the children try hard to be clean and not to spill and spoil things. When we deliberately give them mess to play with they feel free and happy about it and relieved that the adults understand their feelings.

6. When he wants to make something a child gradually learns self-control. If he wants to achieve a particular effect he needs patience and perseverance; he discovers that he must work with the material, not against it, and this means understanding its properties with his mind as well as with his senses. He finds it is worth subduing impatience and carelessness. In time he attains a high standard of self-discipline like every true artist.

7. Although much creative play results in individual achievement, a great deal is done in groups and this helps the social development of each child in the group. He learns to swap ideas, accept criticism and take his turn at doing some of the uncongenial bits of the project.

Imaginative play, make-believe and drama

All of us, adults and children, enjoy dressing-up. Sometimes we disguise our everyday selves by putting on formal clothes or by wearing a uniform or ritual garments. The Services, the Church, Parliament, the Law, set spectacular standards in this. Most of us follow more humbly as Scouts and Guides, or members of the Red Cross or the W.R.V.S. We have all certainly put on special clothes for a wedding or a party. With the clothes we take on also the demeanour and dignity appropriate to them. Sometimes we pretend to be somebody quite different by taking part in a play or an opera or a pageant.

The impulse to 'be' somebody else shows itself very early. By his first birthday the baby is putting his feet into other people's shoes and wearing other people's hats on his head. We use these very expressions in our adult life: 'I wouldn't like to be in his shoes', or 'Under his private hat he does this but when he wears his official hat he must do that'. To practise several roles and to imagine oneself doing somebody else's job are so natural to us that we are not surprised when we see children spending a great deal of time in make-believe play.

But it is more than dressing-up with young children. The period of imaginative play is a vital part of their development and their learning. By playing out different roles they are assuming something of the character and skill of each personality they adopt; they are digesting experiences and they are coming to terms with reality.

Experts call this role-playing by various names, none of which is wholly satisfactory. To call it 'imaginative' play is not quite accurate because a child's play can be imaginative without his 'being' other people. To call it 'dramatic' play is not accurate either, because it suggests an objectively planned and designed performance which does not at all describe the role-play of younger children. To use the phrase 'make-believe' suggests a self-consciousness, almost a deliberately artificial attitude, on the part of the child and this is so far from the truth about the play of young children that some critics consider the phrase to be disrespectful. So it is difficult to know which word to adopt. I have used all three words because they occur in other books and are familiar to all those who work with young children but I use each with reservations. What is essential is that we should recognise the importance of this activity to the little child and regard it with respect.

The children use any of the equipment in the home, nursery or school for their imaginative play but we supply them as well with particular material in the form of clothes, hats and bags for dressing up and some furnishings for house and hospital and shop play. These need not be elaborate. A clothes-horse, draped with a tablecloth or a sheet, put across a corner of the room, or even the space behind the sofa makes a house corner. Supermarkets throw out a great many stout cartons which make excellent tables and beds. I have seen a whole playhouse made by a mother for her two-year-old from two large cardboard packing cases from a supermarket. Since so much make-believe play is based on the doings of home and family most nurseries and infant schools have a permanent house corner (or wendy house) set up. For this a simple screen, some boxes, a table and chairs, teasets, pots and pans, brooms and dustpan, dolls, dolls' clothes and bedclothes, an ironing board and iron, basins, and a looking-glass are enough. Most nursery school staff paint boxes to look like cookers and dressers and these are useful but a sturdy box can do duty for table, chair or doll's bed if necessary and the children will use it for a dozen other things as well. If all the furniture is too realistic or too elaborate it has fewer uses.

The children play a good many games about nurses and doctors so a child-sized bed with blankets is useful in another corner together with some aprons and bottles and perhaps a stethoscope bought in a toy shop or made from tubing and a cotton reel. The children will push the bed into the house corner if they want to play about illnesses at home.

Some nursery schools have a permanent shop corner with a counter and goods made of papier mâché or plaster and bandage. In others children build their own shop when their play demands one. In infant schools a class shop often plays a large part in play leading to mathematics and writing.

'Being' other people

Here are some examples of this kind of play taken from the records of parents, nursery assistants and teachers who have watched children.

(a) P. (14 months) in the day nursery is fond of draping her head and face with cloths.

(b) A mother reported: this morning S. (15 months) came into the kitchen with my hat and one glove on and looked very pleased when she saw I had noticed her.

(c) Nine months later the same mother noted: during the month after her second birthday S. had periods of 'being' different people or things. For instance for a week she was a monkey and always referred to herself as 'monkey'. If I said 'Susan, come and have dinner, dear,' she said, 'monkey come and have dinner'. The next week she was 'Rosey Mary' and the following few days she was 'Soey' (i.e. soldier). Her father and I fell in with her play during this time.

(d) Elizabeth (2 years 6 months, in a day nursery) is carrying her own rag doll about, tucked underneath her arm. She squats down, drops the doll on the floor, picks up a piece of gingham which is lying on the floor and wraps the doll in it, taking a good deal of care. She walks with the doll to a box, bends and drops the doll into the box, head first. Its legs stick up. She stoops as if to do something to it but is distracted by a crash in the house corner and goes over to see what it is. She does not come back.

(e) Kenneth (3 years 3 months, in a nursery school) is sitting in a large cardboard carton. He is wearing a peaked cap and is holding a steering wheel from a car. He moves the wheel round and back making low hissing noises. From time to time he leans over to one side or the other, raising his voice in an 'Ah-ah' sound, swinging the wheel round.

(f) Lucy (3 years 4 months, in a nursery school) is washing dolls' clothes in the house corner, today moved outside into the garden. She has a bowl of water on the table and some soap flakes and is rubbing the clothes very carefully. She hangs each one with pegs on a line stretched between a chair and a post as she finishes washing it. Linda (3 years 5 months) is ironing dolls' clothes near Lucy. She uses an ironing board with a small iron. She spends a lot of time on one doll's dress, turning it round and round on the board. She puts it on a box; takes it up again and irons it again; puts it down again and picks up a jacket. She irons this quickly and puts it down on top of the dress. She begins to iron another dress. She does not talk to Lucy who takes no notice of her.

(g) Benny (3 years 7 months, at a nursery school) is standing in the garden wearing a policeman's helmet. He is making wide gestures and talking to himself. No one takes any notice of him.

(h) Hank (4 years, in a playgroup): 'This is a fire truck. This is a fire truck. Yah!' He scrambles up on the metal support for nesting bridges and sits astride it, yelling. He scrambles down, dashes to the music corner, seizes a triangle and climbs up again. 'This is the bell.' He hits the triangle vigorously, yelling.

(i) A correspondent writes: Two children, a girl and a boy, ages unknown but about 3½ years, were sitting on either side of a table in the wendy house of the United Nations' Nursery School in Geneva. They were both new to the nursery school and could not speak each other's language. For the twenty minutes they were observed they took it in turns, with grave courtesy, to 'pour' from an empty teapot into dolls' cups and to offer a cup to the other. They then drank the imaginary tea and smiled delightedly at each other before reversing roles. I moved away at the end of twenty minutes but the game was continuing.

(j) Nancy and Lorna (both 4½ years, in a nursery school) are working together in the house corner. Nancy wears a long cotton skirt held by elastic at her waist. She is peeling potatoes very slowly (the knife is rather blunt), holding her tongue between her teeth, and is putting them into a saucepan. Lorna is cutting up dandelion leaves and putting them in a colander. She wears an apron and has a scarf tied round her head. They occasionally talk to each other. Nancy puts her saucepan on top of the stove. Lorna tips her leaves into a baking tray and comes to the stove. She stands while Nancy opens the oven and together they put in the baking tray and Nancy closes the oven. Nancy goes back to the table and picks up a handful of potato peelings. She stands undecided. She puts the peelings back on the table and goes away. Lorna gets a broom and sweeps the floor. She sees the teddy bear lying on the floor. She drops the broom, picks up the bear, hits it several times saying 'Don't do that, don't do that. Now go to bed.' She throws the bear on to the dolls' bed and picks up the broom. Nancy comes back with some newspaper. She puts this on the table and puts the potato peelings in it and tries to wrap them up tidily, grunting. Lorna says 'Where will you put them?' Nancy: 'In the dustbin.' Lorna: 'Where in the dustbin?' Nancy: 'Miss X will put them in.'

(*k*) Leslie (3 years 5 months) is lying on a stretcher bed in the nursery school playroom covered with a blanket. Nola (4 years 4 months) stands near the bed in a nurse's apron. Harold (4 years 5 months) stands on the other side. He says: 'It's a sore throat.' Leslie tries to get out of bed. Nola pushes him back. 'You can't get up. You're not allowed to.' (This play went on until dinner time, several other children joining and leaving the group from time to time. There were several different 'patients' but Nola and Harold remained nurse and doctor.)

(*l*) A group of four of the four-year-olds are in the wendy house. Recorder cannot see what goes on. There is a good deal of shouting and scolding. Bob's voice: 'I want my breakfast. Give me my breakfast.' Stanley's voice: 'We can't go to work yet. We haven't had our breakfast.' Carol's voice: 'Get it then.' Bob's voice: 'You've got to get it.' Carol: 'I can't, I'm feeding the baby.' Stanley: 'You don't feed the baby now.' Carol: 'I do.' Bob: 'You don't.' Monica's voice: 'Yes she does. You feed the baby before breakfast.' (Recorder was interrupted at this point but the group in the wendy house went on with the game for most of the morning. It was noisy and there was some swearing and quarrelling.)

(*m*) Josephine (4 years 11 months, in the nursery school field) has a little cart. Mavis (3 years 10 months) helps her to fill it with gravel. She carries it. 'I'm Daddy carrying coal.' Mavis carries a pram with a doll in it: 'I'm Mummy.' Josephine fills the cart again and calls: 'Ice-cream — see it's ice-cream now.' She runs along the path calling 'See the ice-cream' in a sing-song. Valerie (3 years) starts wheeling a very large pram and does so for about 100 metres and then abandons it. Josephine comes up to it and wheels it up the steep slope to the next level in the field. She says, pointing to Mavis, 'She's my Mummy and I'm her little — ' (corrects herself) 'big girl and this is my scooter. Mummy, can I scoot round the sunshade?' (The 'sunshade' is a lacrosse goal on the field.) There is a group of the children in the goal. Irene (4 years 7 months) says 'We're in the sunshade to be out of the rain.' Josephine says 'No, we're in the park and the sun is shining' (it is really a dull day) 'and we're in the sunshade to keep the sun off our faces.' She continually addresses Mavis as 'Mummy'. Irene has a pram without a doll in it but refers to her 'baby' in the pram.

(n) A nursery school teacher reports: 'We have had an outbreak of weddings in the nursery this week. June's auntie was married and June was a bridesmaid and since then she has been organising all the older children and telling them how to play. Miss Y. bought some net to make veils and all the long skirts have been dragged out of the dress-up box. Danny's mother brought a whole box of old artificial flowers and we made some wreaths for their heads and the children made posies. Even the boys have been quite interested.'

(o) An infant school teacher reports: 'In the playground we have the body of an old van which a parent gave us. The children use it constantly. The most popular game seems to be buses. About eight children usually take part and the same two nearly always boss the game — James who is the driver and Faye who is the conductress. They chivvy the others into their places and call out the stops and Faye gives out tickets which she keeps in a bag hung round her neck. No one can get off until James says the bus has stopped. Faye opens the doors at the back and lets them out. Sometimes they are a coach going to the pantomime or the Zoo. It is sometimes a quiet, orderly game and sometimes there is a lot of shouting and bustling.'

These records show in a fragmentary way some of the motifs of the children's imaginative play when they are 'being' other people in familiar situations of home and clinic and traffic. Mothers and fathers, sick children, doctors and nurses, policemen, firemen, bus drivers are all roles they assume and play out.

As one would expect, the play becomes more skilful, more detailed and more vocal as the children grow older. More and more they tend to play in groups as they reach four years and over, but the groups tend to dissolve and reform in the nursery school. They appear to be more permanent in the infant school.

Play with dolls is a good example of how the play develops. The two-year-old is happy with a simple doll and a cloth to wrap it in. The four-year-old demands a more lifelike doll, clothes to put on and take off and proper bedclothes. Both can be content with a box for a bed and if necessary a wheeled cart to push the doll about. They both show tenderness and care in tucking up the doll but the two-year-old is not expert and the doll is sometimes upside down. The six-year-old likes a proper doll's bed with a mattress and demands a pram. The two-year-old will play happily alone and casually with her doll, the four-year-old is often content alone but enjoys having one or two others to join in and puts more detail into the play. The six-year-old likes being one of a steady group and the game may have an elaborate structure.

Most of the games centre round real experiences of the children but we also see a good deal of what we may call secondhand experiences being played out. The children will 'be' people they see on television or at the cinema. We have boys rushing about with a table-cloth tied round their necks crying 'I'm Batman, I'm Batman'. At times the nursery and the infant schools are full of Daleks and cowboys and spacemen.

Building and making

Creative and *imaginative* play are very close and often cannot be separated. A child will build with bricks and then name his building ('a house' or 'a hospital') and work out some play with toys and scraps and imaginary people in and around the building. Groups of children will spend many hours building elaborate structures with planks and boxes and barrels making a drama as they go, altering and adapting the building to meet the needs of the game. A child will dart away from the group to go to the woodwork bench and nail pieces of wood together and dash back to add his contribution to the structure. Another child will go to the paint corner, cut a piece of card to the shape he wants (a crown, a belt, a flag, a signal), paint it and return with it to the group. Another will make objects of clay or plasticine to add to the properties of the group game. In the nursery school one game may go on round a piece of building for several days. In the infant and junior school it may go on for weeks or even all the term. A good teacher will try to make room for erections of blocks at which the children have been working hard to remain undisturbed at least overnight. Some nursery schools have special block play areas where this is possible. Bigger structures are often outside the playroom or classroom, in a corridor or in the garden, so they can more easily remain intact without taking up too much room, but sometimes they have to be tactfully protected from other children, caretakers and maintenance staff.

Here are some more records, this time of imaginative play based on building and making.

(*a*) Joe (2 years 1 month, in the day nursery) is arranging cube blocks very carefully one behind the other in a row on the floor. He is talking to himself in a low voice, unintelligibly to observer. He pulls the first block along away from the others, hesitates, puts his hand on block at the other end of the row and pushes, still muttering something. The blocks move along. He pushes harder, the line of blocks breaks. He says 'Ah' loudly and straightens the row. He pushes again making a sound like 'burr-r-r' but this is not very clear. He stands up and looks round. His foot knocks one of the bricks out of line. He suddenly kicks at the bricks and sends them scattering, shouting as if excited.

(b) Rosemary (3 years 5 months) is reported by her mother to have played for some time with blocks and dolls making the following arrangement and explaining it in detail to her mother.

a large blocks make a bed
b 'sick' doll
c 'doctor' doll
d 'nurse' doll
e a shell said to be a toy
f a pyramid block said to be the light

(c) A nursery school teacher reports: A group of four-year-old boys and a couple of three-year-olds have been making a space ship in the nursery this week. It started as quite a small affair with some of the hollow blocks but it gradually grew. After rest time the first day they went back to it and so I left it overnight. Next morning they were delighted to find it again and started to work on it, adding cartons, a motor tyre and several boards. That

afternoon they covered part of it in with a sheet of thick poly-
thene we keep to protect the floor from clay. They altered its
shape several times and painted parts of it and at the end of the
week it was quite a large project which attracted many of the
other children. It was the centre for a great deal of conversation
and discussion. The development of the space ship theme
seemed logical all the way through. I explained to the group that
we should have to clear it away on Friday afternoon so that the
cleaners could work over the weekend. They accepted this and
made another game of the demolition.

Enclosures   There seems to be an instinct in all children to make
little *enclosures* for themselves. Solitary children will sit under a
table or make a den in a corner behind the piano or the sofa. Groups
of children use anything to hand. A mother writes:

> We have a large empty room in which we store a few things and
> in which the children and their friends are allowed to play on
> wet days. The first thing they always do is to divide the space up
> into smaller areas, with broken chairs, boxes, old curtains, rugs,
> anything they can lay their hands on. It is as if the large room is
> too much for them, they want little spaces they can manage.

For two years we observed the cubby-building of the children in
an Australian boarding school. The school was built in a clearing in
the bush so that trees and shrubs grew close around the buildings.
The numbers in the school fluctuated a little but there were always
between fifty and sixty children between two and twelve years in
the junior section and they spent a great deal of their spare time
making cubbies in the bush. A cubby is a house or den made from
anything available; in this case the shrubs, bushes and trees made
convenient bases for building. In this activity there was a most
obvious division in method among the children, the age of the split
being at about seven years. There were subgroups in the two main
divisions and each subgroup made a cubby.

The younger group (the twos to sevens) built close to the school
buildings, usually under a bush, using bark (which was available in
large strips), stones and dead branches. They were noisy and cheerful
about it, working without adult help but freely inviting and even
coaxing the grown-ups to visit the cubbies when they were finished
and to have tea parties there with them. One constant feature of the
cubbies built by the youngest of the under-sevens groups was a
lavatory, always the first thing to be put into the hut once the walls
and roof were finished. Sometimes it was a circle of pebbles and

sometimes a structure of stones and wood. It was courteously shown
to visitors but we never saw it used. Break-time fruit and biscuits
were often eaten sitting in the cubbies. Otherwise teaparties were
usually imaginary with leaves and bark for cups and saucers and
plates and pebbles or clay or nothing at all for food.

The older children (the sevens to twelves) did their building in
secret. Not only were adults and younger children never invited to
visit but each small gang took great pains to hide its building from
the other gangs. If adults, walking through the bush, came upon a
cubby the inmates stayed hidden inside, quite silent, until they
passed. There appeared to be a good deal of attempted raiding and
protecting of cubbies among the gangs and some fierce battles sometimes broke out but these were never reported to adults, whose only
evidence was the stealthy movements and savage sounds they heard
and subsequent grazes and scratches and bumps they were asked to
minister to at bedtime.

The popularity of cubby-building waxed and waned, the weather,
holidays, the school play and other activities having obvious
influence on it as well as less obvious factors, but it was never
entirely abandoned.

Sand and soil   These are materials for imaginative play as much as
for creative play. We have already discussed play with sand where
the children use it for food and petrol in their games and the older
ones make race tracks, wharves, walls and roads for their games with
Dinky toys. The same kind of games can be played even more
successfully in soil and mud. A group of six boys aged between eight
and ten years at the Australian school where the cubby-building has
been described, spent a week with penknives and sticks carving an
elaborate network of roads, flyovers, tunnels, underpasses, railways
and bridges covering a length of about 4 metres on a clay bank
exposed by the cutting of a road through the school property. It
began modestly and spread logically and deliberately. Each boy had
a number of small wheeled vehicles, mostly Dinky toys and trains,
and the roads and railways were scored out to scale to fit them.
Periods were spent in the movement of traffic only, when descrip-
tions of loads, freight, passengers, timetables, speeds and distances
were woven into the game of an imagined countryside. Then the
need for expansion would lead to periods of excavation and building
with lengthy explanations from one to the other of methods and
reasons and consultations about linking up of efforts. The adults
were never consulted and only knew about the work because they
could watch it from a distance. Quite suddenly the interest flagged

and the work was abandoned but the excavated countryside remained on the bank for another week until a heavy shower of rain wiped it out.

Drama

The imaginative play of young children is real to them because they are still discovering the difference between what is in their own minds and what is outside fact. As they grow older children become conscious of their own identities and are able to watch what is going on around them in a more detached way. They can then decide when to pretend and when to stop and thus make-believe games gradually turn into dramatic play in the adult sense. Six- and seven-year-olds begin to dramatise favourite stories and poems, usually a leader in the group giving sketchy directions and the others speaking their parts as they play. They use the dressing-up clothes and any materials to hand. Gradually these spontaneous plays develop into more carefully planned performances with prepared parts and properties made by the children. Advice and help with the arrangements are sought from adults, tickets and programmes are written out and the audience is organised. Thus, again, in infant and junior schools creative and imaginative play is closely interwoven.

The value of imaginative and dramatic play

We encourage make-believe and imaginative play among the children because we believe it has great value for them and helps them in their development. We can separate out some of the ways in which it is of use if we watch the children as they play.

1. It is fun. They enjoy the feel of swishing long skirts and they like to see how they look in helmets and crowns.
2. It gives them opportunities to practise skills they will use as they grow up. They find out how to do things like pouring and peeling, cutting and cleaning, bandaging and tending, building and stacking, driving and steering, cooking and serving, tidying and sorting, not just as isolated skills but in the appropriate context.
3. 'Being' other people gives children the opportunity to feel like them. Feeling what it is like to be a mother or a doctor or a policeman leads to some understanding of adult roles and responsibilities and the relationships of people to each other.
4. 'Being' other people helps children to sort out reality from

fantasy. At the same time it helps them to understand purpose and the passing of time, to look to the future and to remember the past. To play out a role the player must hold the present situation in his mind while he develops it into the next step.

5. Imaginative play lets each child bring out into the open many anxieties and worries. He can play over experiences that have interested him or made a deep impression on him, such as going on an unusual journey or seeing the demolition of a building. He can live through again at his own pace experiences that have frightened or shocked him, such as a quarrel between his parents or having his tonsils out, until he comes to terms with them. He can recreate ceremonies which he can see are important to adults but which he himself does not understand such as weddings and christenings. All these things become part of his inner life and the next time he experiences the same kind of thing he is better prepared for it.

6. In their make-believe play children can be angry and violent to their dolls and their imaginary characters without doing any harm. Growling and screaming and beating can all be part of the game and so long as no real person is hurt no harm is done. Since they really feel these violent impulses this kind of play is like a safety-valve.

7. Imaginative play and make-believe can be solitary but they can also be a form of communication, as in the incident in the Geneva nursery school already described (p. 64). When the games involve groups as they usually do from 3½ to 4 years onwards they are excellent opportunities for exchanging ideas, taking turns and learning to get on with other people. The children talk freely, discuss and argue. Later such games can lead to a good deal of creative writing.

Learning

When we watch children playing we can see something about how they learn. The young baby learns about the world by exploring things with his mouth but he also learns by the way his mother lifts and touches him, by the tone of her voice and by the way she looks and smiles at him. The toddler learns by his active exploration of his surroundings. He collects facts and practises skills. As soon as he understands what is being said to him he can begin to use language as a tool to learn from the experience of others. When he can talk he can ask questions and later exchange ideas.

At the same time the young child learns by unconsciously absorbing the attitudes and standards and social habits of those closest to him. The way adults do things and the tones of voice in which they say things count more than what is done and said because these reveal the unconscious values of the adults.

Along with these ways of learning, the child is constantly and carefully observing and deliberately copying what the grown-ups do, at first without understanding why they are doing it but later comprehending more and more. His make-believe play helps him to sort out the pattern of behaviour and relationships among the people around him.

When he can read he has at his command all the stored knowledge man has built up and he can soon use the generally accepted symbols of mathematics, maps, music, pictures and diagrams to help him learn more.

Good teachers try to keep a balance between the child's own efforts to experiment and discover for himself and his free use of the inheritance stored for him in books.

Children's learning depends on their maturing and we should know enough about this to provide what they need at each stage. If we give them too little material to play with they will be limited and restricted in their experience and may not discover the patterns and relationships in their world which they need to build on for further learning. If we give them material unsuited to their age and ability they become bored and frustrated. If we do not give them enough time to play and learn at their own pace but are always interrupting them with demands to do something else we may prevent them from following problems to their conclusion and carrying the results on to the next stage of their play. If we do not encourage them and show them that their work is valuable we will destroy their confidence and make them despair of learning. If we hedge them about with too many restrictions and unreasonable prohibitions we will discourage them and make them feel we do not want them to learn. If we are not honest in answering their questions we will not help them to be fearless in finding out the truth of things. In fact, if we do not love them they cannot learn.

We do not understand enough about learning yet to know whether there are periods in the child's development which are critical for his learning but from studies of deprived and handicapped children it does seem clear that children's ability to learn suffers if they do not have certain needs fulfilled at particular stages of development. For example the baby in his first year of life needs someone on whom he can depend for love and encouragement.

Children who have not had someone to love and take an interest in them at this stage are found to be slower and less confident in their capacity to learn. When the baby is ready to move about he needs opportunity for safe exploration and discovery with a loving adult in the background. When he begins to talk he needs people to talk to him and listen to him, with whom he can play word games and hold conversations and when he begins to ask questions he needs willing, honest answers. This is a vital link in the process of his learning. He needs plenty of varied play material and soon he needs other children to play with. When he goes to school he needs a planned environment rich in materials and possibilities, a variety of challenging experiences and satisfying human relationships.

Further reading

Chesters, Gwendolen E., *The Mothering of Young Children*, 2nd edn, Faber, 1956, particularly Chapter 7.

Dean, Joan, *Art and Craft in the Primary School*, 2nd edn, A. & C. Black, 1963.

Dunnett, R., *Art and Child Personality*, Methuen, 1948.

Gardner, D. E. M., *The Education of Young Children*, Methuen, 1956, particularly Chapter 4.

Garvey, Catherine, *Play* (*The Developing Child*, eds J. Bruner, M. Cole and B. Lloyd), Fontana/Open Books, 1977.

Grozinger, W., *Scribbling, Drawing, Painting*, Faber, 1955.

Lowenfeld, Viktor, *Your Child and his Art*, Collier-Macmillan, 1954.

Matterson, E. M., *Play with a Purpose for the Under-Sevens*, Penguin, 1965, particularly Chapters 5 and 7.

Mendelowitz, Daniel, *Children are Artists*, 2nd edn, Stanford U.P., 1963.

Newson, John and Newson, Elizabeth, *Toys and Playthings in Development and Remediation*, Allen & Unwin, 1979.

Opie, I. and Opie, P., *Children's Games in Street and Playground*, O.U.P., 1969.

Richardson, M., *Art and the Child*, University of London Press, 1948.

Roma, Lear, *Play Helps: toys and activities for handicapped children*, Heinemann, 1977.

Simpson, D. and Alderson, D., *Creative Play in the Infants' School*, Pitman, 1950.

Tomlinson, R. R., *Children as Artists*, Penguin, 1944.

Viola, W., *Child Art*, 2nd edn, University of London Press, 1942.

Chapter 4

Adjusting to each other I

The need to adjust

Children often behave in ways which puzzle and concern experienced workers and bewilder and irritate the less experienced. We asked 200 adults working with children to make a list of behaviour which troubled them most. These workers were assistants in day nurseries, Community Homes and nursery schools; playgroup leaders and helpers; and classroom assistants in infant and primary schools.

The items on their lists varied with their age and experience and, of course, with the age of the children they worked with, but when the lists were analysed two items outnumbered all the others — aggression and disobedience. Other things which worried them included temper, pestering for attention, swearing, whining, lying, stealing, eating problems, lack of concentration and a number of personal habits.

These adults were all concerned about their own reaction to the children's difficult behaviour. Most of them admitted that they felt guilty when they were angry or exasperated by what the children did. But at the same time they were sure that children could not be allowed to behave just as they liked all the time if this involved hurting other children, or disturbing the group or endangering themselves. Discussions about these points helped to clear some issues.

We must first distinguish between 'bad' behaviour and behaviour which is only tiresome or inconvenient to the adults. Sometimes a good deal of thought has to be given to this by the adults in charge of any group of children so that they can agree on what they consider reasonable and on what bounds they will set. Once they decide on this they will feel more confident in their attitude to the children and be consistent about their demands.

We are, however, constantly troubled by falling short of our ideals in our day-to-day dealing with children. The calm, affectionate, relaxed attitude which we should like to maintain slips only too easily into irritability or annoyance. We hear our voices growing shrill and feel our tempers growing short. We find ourselves fussing over trifles, getting cross at spills and messes and showing dismay about unimportant accidents to material. This is human and it can be understood and therefore more easily remedied if we think about what is involved.

In each situation there are at least three factors — the children, ourselves and the immediate environment. We react to the children, they react to us and we are both influenced by the environment.

The children are still developing; they are immature and inexperienced. Their feelings are strong and they have not gained control of them yet. Much of each child's behaviour belongs to his stage of development but it is also influenced by his temperament, his abilities, his health, his family, his immediate feelings and his history. His behaviour may be normal for his stage of development or it may be a cry for help. If it is normal we accept it and offer him sensible ways of expressing his feelings. If he is asking for help by behaving outrageously we must let him know we recognise this and do something positive about it. This may mean asking for skilled advice but meanwhile he needs our steady love and support.

We are mature and experienced but no one's upbringing is perfect and we all have pockets of immaturity and childishness left within us. We are, however, capable, if we wish, of standing away from ourselves and recognising these weak spots, accepting them and allowing for them. We may be able to acknowledge that our first reaction to a child's angry attack on us is to be angry ourselves and to want to shout or hit back. If so, then we have not grown up in this part of our emotional life. Once acknowledged it is much easier to deal with. We are also, of course, influenced by our health and by our personal responsibilities and anxieties.

All kinds of things in the *immediate environment* influence us and the children — the weather, the size and furnishing of the room, the temperature and ventilation, the number of people about, the amount of noise and the time of day.

We shall waste less energy if we take practical steps to adjust ourselves and the environment for the child. Sometimes it is sensible to change some part of the routine, or alter the arrangement of equipment to allow for our own weaknesses or to relieve pressure on everyone. One head teacher of a nursery school was irrationally nervous about the conventional wooden-seated swing. She found that she wasted so much energy curbing her anxiety whenever the children used the swing that she had it removed. She gave the children plenty of swinging experiences by providing thick knotted ropes, hanging tyres and several kinds of sling-swings. She felt more relaxed and had more energy to use in constructive ways.

Mastering the play material is energetic and absorbing enough for young children without our making unnecessary difficulties by the way we store or set it out for them. We should try to avoid bottle-necks when we arrange furniture and big equipment so that there is always a clear passage for running, and for pushing and pulling the larger pieces of material and riding the wheeled toys. Bricks, paints and clay should be stored where they can be easily reached and replaced by the children. Arrangements for storing woodwork tools after use should be simple and clearly understood so there need be no frustration for the children and no need for us to be constantly reminding them about it. Dolls' clothes should be strong enough to stand up to frequent tugging and pulling on and off. Any material that is not strong enough for experiment and manipulation is frus-trating and disappointing for the child who is trying to build or make something with it, so all play material in the early years should be strong and sturdy. More delicate material is suitable later on when the smaller muscles of wrists and fingers are mature. Implements should work properly — scissors, although blunt-ended, should really cut, hammers should be heavy enough to hit a nail firmly, saws should be sharp enough for the wood we provide, clamps should really hold the wood steady, the woodwork bench should be the right height, wheeled toys should run easily. This all means careful planning and constant supervision by the adults but prevents a good deal of irritation for the children.

The routine of the day and the material provided should be such that the children are never overtired or overexcited. A child usually has a healthy rhythm of play — vigorous play followed by a period of quieter play. Opportunities for both should always be available so that each child can work to his own rhythm. Periods of waiting for bathroom or meals should be cut to a minimum, story and music periods should be neither too long nor too short, and an advance warning should always be given when we want the children to change what they are doing.

If we know our children well we can often prevent 'bad' behaviour by recognising signs of tension building up and release it by suggesting a change of occupation or skilfully diverting attention to something interesting. We can often prevent situations arising which we know will lead to hostile feelings between particular children.

When a child's behaviour gets out of control or we feel our patience reaching its limit there are some things we can remember which will help us both. They are these:

1. The child deeply needs us to love him and value him. He does not really want to behave badly.
2. He needs us to attend to him, to encourage him and to approve of him.
3. He needs strength in us to protect him against his own violent feelings and to help him achieve balance. An irritable voice shows weakness in us.
4. He needs to know that we have set bounds to his behaviour; to know what they are; and to know that we are in control of the situation.
5. He needs something positive to do.

Aggressive behaviour

Because adults worry so much about violent behaviour in children it may be as well to consider it in some detail.

By 'aggressive behaviour' we found that assistants, helpers and house parents meant behaviour of this kind: physical attacks on other children or on adults, such as hitting, punching, pushing, kicking, biting, pinching, spitting; verbal attacks such as calling names, rudeness, abuse, threats; destruction of property or of other children's work or attacks on play material, including pictures; snatching and grabbing; bossiness, bullying, teasing, interfering; quarrelling, scuffling, rough displays of affection. Some added temper tantrums and screaming to the list.

Everybody can give examples of agressive behaviour. If we try to separate out some of the motives that seem to be behind it this may help us to deal with it when it occurs.

Curiosity and experiment   A certain amount of aggressive or destructive behaviour springs from *curiosity and experiment*. Here is a simple example from a day nursery:

(a) John (6 months) and Shirley (10 months) are on a rug on the floor. Shirley reaches out to grab John's eyes. He shows interest at first then turns his head away and cries. She stops. They exchange gurgles and smiles and reach out towards each other. She gives him a toy and then grabs it again. He grunts as if in protest. She repeats the process and he reacts as before. She then reaches over to him and grabs his arm and shakes it.

Two examples from nursery schools:

(a) Michael (3 years 8 months) discovers that the kitchen scales make an interesting noise and he jerks them up and down violently until the teacher asks him to stop.

(b) Caryl (4 years) is in the sandpit building a castle. Andrew, Gillian and Bryan join her and discuss her castle. She says she is going to build it up to the sky. Andrew (3 years 8 months) says 'I shall destroy it'. Caryl says 'Wait until I put this one [bucketful of sand] on it'. She does so and he comes and pushes the castle down with his hands. The others all smile and Gillian begins to build the sand up again.

The first two of these samples are straightforward. The third is more complex because it is more than just destruction for simple curiosity. Andrew and the others seem not to be quite sure what will happen when the castle, built up with care and hard work, is destroyed. Little children are frightened of their own destructive impulses and need to experiment. In this case they find nothing terrible happens when the castle is pushed over and the sand is there to build up again.

An act of destruction arising from single-minded scientific curiosity had more serious repercussions for two eight-year-old boys who were discovered cutting up the seat of a bus with a pocket knife. The conductor and the driver were very angry and the children were dumb with fright. At the police station they could give no explanation and even after their parents came they were still silent. A kindly policewoman took them aside and said she was sure that they had a sensible reason for what they had done. They broke down and explained that they were responsible for a pet mouse belonging to their class at school. They had heard that bus seats were made of rubber and they needed a cube of rubber to put in the mouse cage to find out whether their mouse could bounce.

Most material in nurseries and schools is tough enough to withstand investigation and that is partly what it is there for. Of course we cannot allow small children to hurt each other or to destroy public property while they are investigating, but we can offer other, more acceptable, opportunities for exploring instead of just scolding the children or removing the object of their investigation. Some young children kick or hit others because they have not met many other children before and do not know how to approach them. In this case and in the case of possible hurt to property we have to make it clear that we understand their need to find out and that we will help them, but that some ways of doing it are not appropriate and cannot be allowed. We can then suggest some positive experimental activity. We must make sure that we have a rich variety of materials for exploration and discovery and that the children have plenty of opportunity and time to use it. We should be constantly reviewing our material and adding to it and we can make sure that we are ready with suggestions at the right moment — 'Have you seen these rollers Miss X brought today?' 'Will you help me to unpack this box of things, please?'

Threatened security   Children sometimes become aggressive when their *security is threatened*. We find this when a child struggles and hits out on parting with his mother at the nursery school; or when in the residential nursery a child kicks the furniture, or is stubborn and contrary when the member of staff he expects at that time does not come on duty; or when a child flies into a rage at a clinic or surgery when the doctor he has learned to trust suddenly hurts him.

A nursery assistant reports:

> Mary (2 years 11 months) has been coming to the nursery for five months and is quite 'settled'. But every morning she clings to her mother and kicks and screams when she is left with me. I hold her quietly and after about six or seven minutes she finds a child to play with and goes off.

When Mary first came to the nursery she probably felt a real threat to her security when her mother left her. By now her kicking and screaming have probably become a kind of ritual, a part of the accepted routine, and this seems to be recognised by the nursery assistant who gives her the necessary support over the bridge period.

In cases where it is clear to us that the child's security has been threatened and he is reacting to his anxiety by being aggressive we know how to act. We comfort him and explain as well as we can what has happened and give him something hopeful to look forward to: 'Mummy will come back when we've had dinner', or 'This is the day Nurse Mary goes to do her shopping. When you wake up in the morning she will be here to help you get dressed'. It is more difficult for us when we suspect his aggression comes from anxiety but don't know what he is anxious about. All we can do then is to give him steady reassurance by not letting his aggression disturb us and by encouraging him to do things which will build up his confidence in himself and our regard for him. We must use our imagination and try to see how it seems to him.

Hitting or pushing is often a simple reaction to being startled or interrupted. When he is older a child can use words to release his feelings in these circumstances but the little child is not yet ready with words. Compare these two examples, given by a nursery nurse and a classroom assistant.

(a) Henry (3 years) joins a group at the mirror in the bathroom. Joan (3 years) accidentally bumps him and he hits her. Joan pushes him away and he pushes her harder. She cries and an adult intervenes.

(b) One of the boys accidentally jogs the arm of Mary (6 years) while she is writing. Mary slams her pencil down and yells 'Now look what you've made me do! That was my very best writing.' She begins to cry and the teacher says, 'You can start a fresh page. It was an accident'.

In the first case blows and pushes were the only way the children could express shock and resentment. In the second case Mary's feelings were just as strong as Henry's but she could use words to express her grief and fury and did not have to hit out. Usually the adults can help in most cases of this kind by a matter-of-fact explanation.

Sometimes we are astonished at the restraint and control shown by young children who are attacked, whose play is interfered with or whose friends are threatened. Here are two examples from the same nursery school:

(a) Kenneth (3 years) comes up to an adult helper with a handful of little horses. He seems delighted to find that one is bigger than the others. At the adult's suggestion he stands them all up on the floor. Michael (3 years) comes up and listens to the conversation between the helper and Kenneth. Then he knocks the biggest horse over. Kenneth stands it up again, turns to Michael, taps him lightly on the shoulder and says 'Now don't knock it over again.' Michael goes away.

(b) A boy and his two sisters are all at nursery school. Arthur (3 years) attempts to bite Mavis (4 years). Josephine (5 years) who is standing beside Mavis says 'Don't you bite her' and smacks his head gently.

Possession   This seems to be another focal point for aggression and hostility. Desire to guard one's own possessions and to take what he has got from someone else leads to grabbing, hitting, screaming and quarrels from babyhood onwards into adulthood, the methods becoming subtler and more sophisticated, although it is surprising how often crude snatching and grabbing crops up all the way along the years.

This is the kind of thing we find in the nursery school.

(a) Doris (2½ years) comes up to a nursery assistant who is making notes and demands to be allowed to write. She is very determined about it. The assistant says 'Not now. I have to write now', but Doris snatches the pencil saying 'I've took it', and scribbles. The assistant says, 'May I have it? I must do my work.' Doris gives it up.

(b) Kenneth (3 years 4 months) arrives with his mother. He runs up to Bernard (3 years 8 months) who has brought his own aeroplane. He tries to take the plane away from Bernard. His mother distracts his attention with a book but when she goes he follows Bernard into the cloakroom and stands watching him. Kenneth's attention is caught by the arrival of some of the other children but soon he sees Bernard with his aeroplane across the room and goes over to look at it. Bernard hides the aeroplane behind his back until Kenneth's attention is diverted to Janet's teddy bear. Five minutes later Kenneth again goes up to Bernard and looks at the aeroplane. Bernard clutches it firmly. Kenneth gets another aeroplane from the toy shelves and throws it across the room. When the teacher asks him to go and pick it up he does so and then for the next twenty minutes he plays with trains and blocks. He then goes outside to the swing. While he is swinging Bernard comes up, still clutching his aeroplane, and demands a swing. A nursery assistant says, 'When Kenneth has had his turn you can have a swing.' Kenneth makes no demur about giving up the swing and the assistant says to Bernard 'Will you let Kenneth hold your aeroplane while you are having your swing?' Bernard says 'No' very firmly and clutches the plane all through his turn on the swing.

(c) Lesley (3 years 8 months) is playing with a train. Brian (4 years) comes up, kneels beside her and touches the train. She screams 'Don't touch it, it's mine'. He goes off.

(d) Gillian (4 years) has a flag. Jan (4 years) comes up and tries to tear it away from her. She sits on the floor and they struggle. The teacher interferes and Jan, going off, kicks Gillian hard.

We are not told what the teacher did but it could not have been perfectly satisfactory since it left Jan feeling hostile and belligerent.

(e) Richard (5 years) and Andrew (4 years 9 months) are building with their bricks. Richard has two arches and Andrew wants one. Richard stubbornly refuses to give him one so Andrew grabs it, knocking a few of Richard's bricks down. Richard cries and knocks down all Andrew's bricks, whereupon Andrew knocks down the rest of Richard's. They then start fighting but later settle down to play with all the blocks together.

During the infant school years there is a good deal of snatching and a good deal of jealous protection of private property. A five- or six-year-old may fly into a passion when another child takes his pencil, crayon or book, even by accident. During the junior school years grabbing is often a group activity — one gang stealing from another.

Of course the baby understands nothing about property or the rights of possession; he is not clear even about his own identity or that of other people. The nursery years are the period when he begins to learn about these things and about the rules of behaviour which surround the ownership of property in our society. By the time he goes to school he is beginning to be sure of his own identity as a person. His possessions are a part of himself, so that if they are attacked he himself is assaulted and he fights back ruthlessly. This is a natural reaction and the other side of the coin is the value he rightly places on his lending or giving or sharing his possessions. He is often generous and eager to lend his things to other children and in doing so is truly giving of himself.

There is no doubt that at any age we are attracted by something that has value to someone else. Sometimes a toy which he has ignored or not even consciously noticed before suddenly seems to have great possibilities to a child when he sees another child playing with it and he immediately wants to try it out. This is a situation we often have to deal with in the playgroup or the nursery and it is one which requires tact and understanding. In the primary school the same situation often arises but here more often the children can use language to discuss the material instead of just grabbing. Of course, being attracted to what is interesting to someone else is the basis of a great deal of education. Children want to read or write or find out about numbers because they see other people finding these things deeply interesting and important. So we should not be too much disturbed by little children snatching or interfering with each other's play but try to protect both sides if we can — the grabber from being snubbed without hope and the possessor from unfair loss; neither is really to blame and each needs comfort although of a different sort. In fact, except where there is real injustice or the snatcher is much bigger than the other child, we need rarely interfere, the children can usually be left to settle the matter themselves.

When we feel we must intervene we have to be careful. It is not much use our just going up to the grabber and taking the toy from him. This only convinces him that the stronger you are the more right you have to grab. If four-year-old Tom snatches her train from two-year-old Mary we have both children to think of. We can say, 'Tom, Mary had the train first. If you want that one very badly find her another train and ask her if she will use that and let you have this one. If she wants to keep this one I'll help you to find one as much like it as we can. There are some on the shelves.' If he won't then we have to think again and make another positive suggestion. He must not be allowed to run off with the train, but neither should we wrest it from him. At the same time Mary may need a reassuring arm round her.

Frustration   Young children often become angry and aggressive *when they are thwarted*. A child wants to do something and to do it now, at once; we forbid it, or we say, 'Later, not now'. Or he knows what he wants to do and he can't manage it — his fingers can't make the scissors work, or the doll's legs won't fit into the pants, or he can't push the barrel up the slope. His exasperation at these obstacles to his wishes takes the form of screaming or stamping or throwing things about. Sometimes he loses all control and flies into a temper tantrum.

We deal with physical expressions of this kind many times in the nursery and playgroup but less often in the infant school where outrage can be expressed verbally or where children sometimes show feelings of resentment quietly by sulking or by muttering or by weeping sadly by themselves.

Here are some of the examples given by parents, nursery assistants and classroom helpers.

(*a*) David (9 months) is taken on to his mother's lap for his evening meal. He makes anticipatory gurgles at the sight of the food. His mother finds it is too hot and she has to wait till it cools before giving it to him. He screams, goes red in the face and kicks with his legs. He suddenly urinates on his mother's lap.

This is an example of the thwarting of a baby's natural eagerness and appetite which need not have taken place with better planning. This is easy to say but it is not so easy for a busy mother or nurse to avoid situations like this from time to time. So long as she realises that she has outraged his 'here and now' expectations of satisfaction and that it is impossible for a baby to understand and accept delay of this kind she can ignore his kicks, comfort him and make up for his disappointment as fast as she can.

(*b*) A staff-nurse in a day nursery reports: We came back from our usual little walk in the park this morning just before dinner. We began to go inside. Duncan (19 months) suddenly sat down on the path and said, very firmly, 'No'. I left him and took two other babies inside and came back for Duncan. I said 'Come on, Dunkie, time for dinner', but he began to crawl away very fast. I picked him up and he screamed and kicked me and spat at me all the way in to the bathroom, and sobbed and struggled while I took his coat off. When I washed his face he tried to bite me and kept writhing and kicking until we got into the nursery where dinner was set out. When he saw the other children sitting there he quietened down and later on ate a good dinner.

Once he can get about, a baby of sixteen months or so begins to be independent. He wants to do things by himself and in his way. He doesn't always know what he wants to do but he knows he doesn't want to do what we want him to. So he becomes awkward and obstinate. We can avoid head-on collisions with him a good deal of the time by distracting his attention or by arranging things his way as often as we can but there are times when he has to do what we want and at these times the resulting behaviour can be tiresome. We have to keep calm and steady and good humoured and just get on with the job as gently as we can. He hates us fiercely while he kicks and screams but these feelings are not pleasant for him and he needs us to go on loving him.

(*c*) A nursery school assistant says: Yesterday we were handing round pieces of apple to the children. Nigel (just 3) took two pieces, one larger than the other. When I asked him to put one back he refused. I took the larger piece from him. He cried angrily 'I want two pieces' several times. I asked him to sit down at the table and he did so but shouted angrily 'I want a big piece'. I said 'That is a big piece' but he shouted 'It isn't' and threw it across the room.

Nigel's sense of justice seems to have suffered a blow. He wanted two pieces so he took them. He is not old enough to understand sharing out among a number of children, he can only think of what he wants and he can't bear it when the adult stops him having it. It was unfortunate that the nursery assistant happened to take the larger piece from him, it made the injustice seem worse. It is probable that Nigel's outburst was the culmination of a series of incidents that he interpreted as ill treatment and his resentment may have been building up. Perhaps his mother was tired and cross at breakfast, or an older child in the family had made him feel foolish and clumsy, or the morning at the nursery had been full of small frustrations and irritations. It is usually unwise to treat an outburst of this kind as complete in itself — it is often a symptom of a bigger load of frustration and resentment. If we understand this we can deal with it more helpfully. It is important to *show* fairness to all children as well as to *be* fair, to take time to explain and demonstrate one piece to each child and to ask the offended child to help give them out if he can bring himself to do this. If he can't then we can only leave him to watch and go on with the next step, and gradually help him to unwind.

(*d*) Another nursery worker gives this example: Workmen came to the nursery to do an emergency job on a chimney. They had a long ladder to the roof and we put this out of bounds to the children who, of course, were interested in the operation. Billy (3 years) and one or two others persisted in trying to climb the ladder and were reminded several times that it was not the children's ladder. We explained that it was needed by the men. To help them remember we put a big semi-circle of boxes and blocks round the bottom of the ladder and we hung an extra ladder on the climbing frame for them. I turned my back for a minute and then I found Billy well on his way up the workman's ladder. I lifted him down and carried him inside. He screamed, kicked, bit and punched me and flew into a tantrum which lasted a long time.

How well we can sympathise with Billy. This was an irresistible temptation to an enterprising and curious boy and he can only have interpreted the adult's treatment of him as an arbitrary thwarting because he was too young to comprehend explanations of danger. His single mindedness, ignoring the blandishment of the extra children's ladder, would have been praiseworthy in other circumstances and if this trait is rightly handled Billy may become a most useful member of society. On the other hand he could not be allowed to climb the dangerous ladder.

It is important to treat a child in a temper tantrum of this kind in the right way. He is best taken away from the other children until the tantrum wears itself out but he should not be left alone because this will frighten him. The physical intensity of his feelings of impotence and rage is terrifying and he will also be afraid that he has destroyed our love for him. So we should stay quietly nearby and when the tantrum is over and he is exhausted he can best be helped by a matter-of-fact suggestion of something to do. We can say, 'Will you come and help me put out the tools (or set out the mugs or tidy up the books)?' It may help him if we wash his face first; this gives us a chance to show him by warm comforting gestures that we still love him. Some children vomit during a tantrum and then, of course, they need very gentle help and comfort. It is a mistake to mention the temper — it wasn't pleasant and he has lost face by being uncontrolled anyhow.

(e) A playgroup leader gives this example: Cathy (4 years) was shown how to tie a bow and was practising on the sash of her doll's dress. She could not get it right and after a while she threw the doll away and stamped up and down furiously.

We all feel like Cathy at times although we have learned not to stamp and shout about it. Some of us swear or take it out on other people by snapping at them. Only the more mature of us can keep our temper and persevere. So when this kind of thing happens in the school or nursery a useful thing to do is to say, 'I know how you feel. Have you tried it this way?' If he doesn't want to try again just then ask him to do something he does well so that he ends up by feeling successful. Or it may be better not to do anything at the moment — we don't always have to intervene.

(f) A classroom assistant gave this unusual example: A class of five- and six-year-olds had just been asked to start clearing away everything on their tables ready for their break. They were being very noisy and several times the teacher asked them to be quieter. She had to ask some of the children several times to put their things away. One girl was told three or four times and at the last time she suddenly turned quite white, her eyes flamed and she screamed out 'Shut up!' to her teacher. The whole class was stunned into complete silence.

This seems to be a case where frustration and irritation have been building up resentment in the child for a long while. It was probably healthier for this child to say 'Shut up' to her teacher than to bottle up her resentment so that she had to express it in bullying younger children or stealing or growing into the kind of person who holds a permanent grudge against society. It sounds as if the teacher for some reason was not fully in control of the class that morning. In any case, however, she did the right thing. The assistant who reported the incident went on to say that the teacher took a deep breath and said, 'Look here, we seem to have been getting on top of each other today. I've felt like saying "Shut up" to all of you this morning. Let's go outside. When we come in again we'll have singing. I've found a new song for us.'

Rivalry often leads to aggression. Parents have to deal with jealous feelings among their children at all ages. In the nursery and play-group we see children pushing each other about in their efforts to use material, or trying to exclude a rival from a game. In the infant school we have to deal with a certain amount of pushing to be first and an eagerness to show work. This is quite natural but it can lead to interference with quieter children and to physical hurt. Later, in the junior school years, rivalry is seen mostly between groups or gangs and leads to scuffling and wrestling, usually quite harmless. Sometimes there is intense rivalry between two children over the leadership of a group. We may see this as fighting or it may take the form of taunting or name-calling or hurtful criticism. Bossiness and jealous attacks on other children and their work seem to appear in all age groups.

The following examples are from records kept by assistants in nursery schools and playgroups.

(a) A student is sitting in the nursery playroom making notes. Elizabeth (3 years 1 month) asks to be allowed to write. She is given the pencil and book. Caryl (4 years 4 months) is watching and asks for a turn. Elizabeth says 'No' but the student suggests that she should have one more turn and then give the pencil to Caryl. Elizabeth does this but as soon as Caryl begins to write she tries to wipe out her scribbles as fast as Caryl makes them and angrily tries to push away the pencil.

(b) Gillian (4 years 2 months), Andrew (3 years 8 months) and Bryan (4 years) are playing inside the wendy house. Philip (4 years 2 months) comes up with a bucket of sand and puts it through the window saying 'Here's some oil for you'. He climbs through the window. Andrew objects to his coming in and there is a scuffle in which Philip puts his sand down Andrew's neck. Andrew cries loudly. A helper comes and helps Andrew to get the sand out of his clothes but he refuses to rejoin the group.

Later in the morning Philip is in the wendy house. Andrew comes up calling 'Let me in'. Philip tries to push him out. There is a scuffle and Andrew hits Philip saying 'I won't come to this school another day'. Gillian comes up to them and the scuffling ceases, all three settling down amiably.

(c) Norman (4 years 7 months) and Michael (3 years 7 months) are playing with wooden trains which fit together. Michael quietly finds out how to fit them. Norman keeps upsetting his arrangement and trying to make Michael do it his way.

(d) Jean (4 years 8 months) is helpful and useful to the younger children during the afternoon but when she realises an adult is watching she becomes officious and bossy and annoys the younger ones.

Here are two examples of aggression in the infant school which seem to arise from rivalry:

(a) In a group of five- to seven-year-old children there is a group of five boys round the rocking horse. A new little boy is having a ride and his twin brother is waiting for a turn. The leader of the group is an older boy. He is doing all the organising of the younger children by telling them when it is their turn and by pushing the horse for them. All goes well until another boy tries to push the horse. The leader tells him to go away and they begin punching each other. The intruder goes off but the incident seems to have upset the children and they wander away leaving the leader riding the horse by himself.

(b) Carol (8 years) stands watching a group of children playing together. She is not included in the game. She goes up to the nearest child and slaps her very hard. The child hits her back and Carol slaps her again.

There is nothing unusual about these examples. We find this kind of behaviour constantly occurring among children. Children must find their own place among their companions. They have a natural impulse towards self-assertion and a desire for power in a world where the odds are so greatly in favour of the strong, efficient adults. If we watch to see that no child is really hurt and that the weaker children get their fair share of opportunity to use equipment and material, there is rarely any need to intervene. We should, however, watch a child who seems constantly moved by jealousy towards another child or who is constantly left out and feels hurt and resentful. This child needs us to build up his self-confidence in any way we can, not by singling him out for special treatment but by seeing that he has opportunities to prove that he is a useful member of the community. Fred was one such child of eight years in a boarding school. He was developing aggressive manners because he was clumsy and his movements were uncoordinated and the other children almost always left him out of group activities. During the making of a class puppet-play the teacher discovered he could roar like a lion most convincingly. She unobtrusively arranged that the jungle scene in the play should be lengthened and more jungle noises put in. The result was that Fred not only became lion-roarer but gradually took over almost all the sound effects for the play and did so well that he became an indispensable member of the group and was accepted without question.

Many classroom assistants in infant schools say that tale-telling among five- and six-year-olds worries them. It is fairly common at this age and is probably mostly a form of rivalry and can be treated as such a matter-of-fact response. It may, however, be a form of testing the adult to see what kind of behaviour she will accept and what disturbs her. It means that the child is not sure of adult standards and is using other children's behaviour to test them. This child may find that family standards and school standards do not match. If this is the case we can at least make sure by our consistent behaviour that he understands school standards and almost certainly the teacher will make special efforts to cooperate with his parents.

Seemingly purposeless aggression   Hardest of all for the adults to accept is *aggressive behaviour for which there seems to be no immediate reason*. It seems to spring from sudden impulse. We can find a great many examples in the records kept by nursery assistants and classroom helpers. Here are some of them:

(a) Sidney (1 year 7 months) is standing in the middle of the floor weeping. Norman (1 year 11 months) comes up and pushes him over. Later Sidney is again standing crying. Jimmy and George (1 year 8 months and 1 year 7 months) are pushing a chair along and run into him deliberately.

(b) Kitty (2 years 2 months) is a happy soul and has been coming to the day nursery for over a year. But she has been biting some of the other children and nurses lately. Today, for instance, she was standing near Dick, who is eighteen months, and she suddenly bit his hand quite sharply. He cried and I picked him up and said, 'That hurt Dick. We'll have to wash it for him. Come into the bathroom.' I let Kitty turn on the tap and we bathed Dick's hand and comforted him.

(c) During dinner John (3 years 4 months) suddenly says loudly to his neighbour, 'Miss —— [the teacher] is a silly old cow.' Both laugh and he repeats it. The other child says, 'Miss —— is a silly old cow-milk.' Much laughter by both children.

(d) Peter (3 years 5 months) is looking at a book. When he turns to a picture of wooden Dutch dolls he squeals and hits the picture several times. He asks an adult helper 'Why is she [pointing to one of the dolls] hitting him?' The helper explains that the dolls are playing leap-frog and jumping over each other. Peter is very much interested and asks for the explanation several times. He then explains to another child that the doll is jumping over another doll and will hit its head. He slaps it again and gets very excited.

(*e*) During a music period Jean (4 years) takes great delight in violently pushing Arthur (3 years) who is marching in front of her so that he stumbles.

(*f*) Gillian (4 years 8 months) passes the table on which are standing small models of houses and traffic signals which the children have been making. She stops, pushes them all over with a grunt of pleasure, and goes on.

(*g*) Rosemary (5 years) is talking to an adult about a new home the family are soon to move to where they will be reunited with their father after his long absence. She describes some of the features of the new house. The adult says, 'When you go back to Daddy you'll . . . ' Rosemary (interrupting) 'I know what I'll do. I'll cut Elizabeth open and take out her heart and throw it away.' Elizabeth is her younger sister. She has not often shown jealousy of her.

(*h*) We have a seven-year-old boy at school who is always doing something destructive such as pulling heads off flowers, or breaking the other children's things. He waits until another child has made something (a tent, a clay model, a brick building) and then he either kicks or knocks it over.

(*i*) There is a girl of eight years old in our class who continually hits other children. She puts her hands around children's throats, usually smaller children than herself. Most of the children are frightened of this girl.

(*j*) Today I was quite frightened. Miss X and I were on duty in the playground and a group of eight- and nine-year-old boys who had been playing rather noisily in a silly kind of way suddenly seemed to go berserk. They ran about knocking the children over and shouting. When they got to the sandpit they began throwing the sand about, screaming with laughter and frightening the younger ones. I didn't know what to do and called out to Miss X to go and get Mr Y (the headmaster) while I gathered some of the frightened ones round me.

It is not only on isolated occasions that children show seemingly purposeless aggression. Children seem sometimes to be in an unhappy mood for a great part of the day for no obvious reason. During this time they may be aggressive and violent to people and things. Here are two accounts from assistants:

(*k*) A large, painted wooden soldier is standing on the floor. Michael

(3 years 8 months) comes up, sees it, and deliberately hits it over. Later he takes a rubber ball from the cupboard, throws it on to the floor and stamps on it a number of times. He says something in a vicious tone with each stamp until the teacher comes and says, 'Take care of it. Michael.' He picks it up and she returns it to the cupboard. He finds it difficult to settle down to play but after trying several things he plays with a train. Then he goes to watch Dennis who is building bricks up at a table. Michael suddenly knocks over the pile and runs away laughing. He begins to play with Bernard with a wooden train but bosses him and dominates the play. He sees John with a little wagon full of blocks and runs up and tries to take it away from him until the teacher comes up and stops him.

(*l*) Charlie (3 years 4 months) and some of the others have spades in the sandpit. Charlie goes up and hits John with his spade. He then finds Mickey digging a hole and goes up and hits him. When an adult helper asks him not to do this he first tries to snatch Mickey's spade and when the helper explains that they each have a spade he tries to push Mickey away and go on digging in Mickey's hole. The helper suggests he come and dig a hole in another corner. He does so but sees Ivor's book lying on the side of the sandpit. He looks at it and then throws it away. He fills in his own hole. After some more work he throws a spadeful of sand at one of the other children, empties his bucket and throws it away. It lands near the helper and when he goes to get it she plays with him. He seems to get much pleasure out of smoothing and patting a little mound but later kicks it away. The helper is by now helping another child to dig a hole and Charlie sits down, puts his feet into the hole and says, 'This is my hole.' He is encouraged to dig one of his own. After dinner Charlie shows off a great deal before some visitors.

We feel helpless and bewildered at destructive behaviour of this kind because we can't see any obvious reason for it. We think 'Why on earth should Gillian knock over the little toys? What was it about them that could have aroused such an impulse in her?' 'Whatever made Peter want to smack the picture so viciously?' 'Why is Charlie so difficult today? Nothing in the nursery routine is different from usual.' These things are hard to understand because we like to know the reasons for things that happen; we have logical minds and illogical behaviour worries us. This is because we have forgotten how different the world appeared to us when we were very young.

The young child has very strong feelings. He is possessed, shaken and driven by them whether they are love, hate, jealousy or fear. He also has a strong sense of urgency because he can't comprehend the passing of time — what he wants he wants now, at once. He is aware all the time of his own smallness and weakness and he is confused about why things happen and about how the real world is managed. Because of this he spends a great deal of his time living in fantasies in which he relives experiences and works out explanations for them. In many of his fantasies he feels powerful, good and clever. Sometimes he gets so frustrated and furious when he is thwarted or when he is jealous that his fantasies are like magic and he wishes to kill or hurt the people who have angered him (like the powerful wishes that are given to people in fairy stories). His fantasy wishes are so strong that he really believes for a while that he *has* killed or hurt them. Since it is the people he loves most that he feels the strongest hatred towards (because their behaviour moves him most), he then becomes anxious and frightened that he has really killed them, because he couldn't bear to be without them, he needs them so much. He has to be reassured that they are safe and still love him.

When a child bites, like Kitty in the record (*b*) on p. 90, it may well be a mixture of hostility and love ('I love you so much I could eat you all up') or it may be a wish to destroy a rival. In any case the helper had to do three things — stop Kitty hurting Dick, explain that biting does hurt badly and then help her to repair the damage by doing something for Dick's hand.

Gradually the child grows able to control his hostile feelings towards people he loves but he still feels full of fury and frustration at times so he gets relief by kicking or hitting something or someone else like his toys or even a perfect stranger. When we see a child like Gillian knocking over the playthings for no apparent reason we know that she is using them as a substitute for someone she wants to hit. It is a good thing she can find something as harmless as this to do to use up her hostility. It is best to make no comment on most of these incidents except perhaps to suggest in a matter-of-fact way that she should help to pick them up. When we see a child throwing his teddy-bear or doll about and smacking it, it is wisest to say nothing: he is drawing off his aggression against someone. Sometimes it helps a child to talk about whatever has aroused his anxiety or anger as in the case of Peter above, who was excited by a picture. Putting things into words often helps to lower the tension but our remarks and answers should be factual and calm.

In a community home the staff often have to cope with children who have nightmares and frightening dreams and wake screaming. Parents have to deal with this, too. It is tiresome but the child is passing through a period of growth in the struggle to deal with his aggression. His dreams, though frightening, are a step towards control. He needs gentleness when he wakes and time to adjust to the safe reassuring world before he falls asleep again.

If the child becomes too self-controlled when he is angry the pressure may build up inside him and we may have one of those seemingly senseless outbursts of destruction or temper that worry us. I knew a four-year-old girl in a residential nursery who was on the whole very 'good' and quiet. She played mostly by herself. But about once a week she would suddenly begin to scream for no apparent reason and go on and on until she was exhausted. Matron discovered that what helped her most was to pick her up and carry her quietly to her own office and put her gently on the floor facing a corner of the room with some blocks or dominoes or Dinky cars to play with while Matron worked at her desk. It seemed that being always with so many other children in the playroom built up some unbearable strain in this little girl which became uncontrollable and burst out into screaming. The corner of the room must have made her feel safe and Matron quietly going about her work brought the world back to normal again. Perhaps if she had been vigorous and active in her play like some of the other four-year-olds, running, hammering, pounding, lifting and pushing she could have used up so much energy and hostility that she would not have built up a burden of anxiety as she did. But some children do not seem able to play like this.

As the children grow and learn more and can make and build skilfully, and as they work out problems of all kinds through their make-believe play they gradually come to terms with their aggressive feelings and use the energy to attack problems of working, discovering and making in school and in playing games. If a child of nine or ten behaves like three-year-old Charlie in the example (*l*) p. 92, we are alarmed because we expect more control by that age. Something has gone wrong and we look for skilled help for the child. Something of this sort must have been the case with the girl of eight years in example (*i*) p. 91. The staff usually discuss such cases and the teacher responsible consults parents and experts.

Summing up on aggression

We have been talking in this chapter mostly about aggression in the form of acts of destruction and hostility seen in young children, but it is more than that. An aggressive drive is part of the equipment we are born with. Without this drive we should have little energy or enterprise. The newborn baby needs it to overcome his helplessness and seek the mother's breast; it is what makes the child persist in his long struggle to gain control of his body and master the skills he needs for living; the scientist and the artist need it to overcome obstacles in the way to their achievement. This spring of energy takes little heed of other people and may cause us to hurt or destroy them. But we are also born with strong feelings of love and the process of growing up is partly the process of finding a balance between our aggression and our love towards the people around us. This takes a long time and we spend most of our childhood and adolescence getting there.

It is our responsibility, when we work with children, to help them to achieve this balance between their aggression and their love. If we have not achieved it securely ourselves we may be disturbed by the violent behaviour of the children instead of accepting it as a natural part of their development.

It does not help to pretend that aggressive feelings and the desire to destroy are not part of the child. They *are* part of him and will remain part of him always and it is our responsibility to give them expression in ways which help him to deal with them and use them constructively. We can do this in several ways.

First we give him steady love however 'naughty' or obstinate or tiresome he is. We should be genuine about this; if we are only acting he senses it at once and feels unsafe. We try to be consistent in our behaviour towards him because he is not clear about what is real and factual in the world and what is part of the imagery in his mind and our consistent behaviour helps him to sort this out. Sensible and reasonable control helps him by making him feel safe.

Then we give him the material and the opportunity to use his energy and to find out that attacking and destroying can lead to making and building. Hammering, sawing, pounding, digging, cutting and tearing lead to interesting and valuable results. We have already mentioned the restoring effects of creative play (see p. 60). We also encourage him to explore and discover things for himself.

We take his make-believe play seriously. We give him time and opportunity for it and never make the mistake of laughing at it or making him feel silly or ridiculous.

We try to make sure children in our care are never bored, whatever their age is. Boredom leads almost always to destructive behaviour or to apathy, or to wasteful day-dreaming.

There are times when we have to act firmly. We cannot allow children to hurt other children or themselves or us, or to destroy other people's property wantonly. There is no point in setting bounds to freedom unless they are necessary and reasonable but then they must be observed. Whatever we decide to do must be done without ill humour and without any sense of retaliation.

It sometimes happens that a group of children will become imbued with a kind of mass excitement and run wildly about. This can happen in the nursery and the infant school (a badly organised music-and-movement period is often an opportunity for this kind of rowdy behaviour) but it is more serious with older children because they are stronger and can do more damage. Even sensible children sometimes suddenly seem to go mad in a group. It is as if they felt no responsibility for their own behaviour but had surrendered to mob control. Firm, swift and strong measures are needed in a case of this kind — the classroom assistant, for example, in paragraph (j) p. 91, sent for the headmaster.

Further reading

Chaloner, Len, *Feeling and Perception in Young Children*, Tavistock, 1963.

Isaacs, Susan, *Social Development in Young Children*, Routledge, 1933.

Isaacs, Susan, *Troubles of Children and Parents*, Methuen, 1948.

May, D. E., *Children in the Nursery School*, University of London Press, 1963, Bristol Univ. Inst. of Educ. Pubns.

Peters, Jocelyn, *Growing Up World*, Longman, 1966.

Winnicott, D. W., *The Child, the Family and the Outside World*, Penguin: Pelican, 1964, particularly Part Three, 35.

See also publications of British Association of Early Childhood Education and of National Children's Bureau.

Chapter 5

Adjusting to each other II

Disobedience and defiance

It is a good thing that children do not obey us all the time: it would be bad for both sides. They would grow up timid and unenterprising and we should become tyrants who never reassessed ourselves and our methods.

But adults find disobedience tiresome and they complain about it a good deal: 'He just waits until we ask for quiet for grace and then he starts stamping, singing, shouting or banging his heels on the floor (3 years).' 'Every day she refuses to come in to dinner. She stands on top of the climbing frame and won't come down (4 years).' 'She always has to be told more than once to do anything and sometimes she'll argue with me till she's in tears (5 years).' 'He will not help to set the tables when he's asked to (5 years).' 'He just pretends not to hear when we speak to him (6 years).' 'They will run on the grass bank when they know they're not allowed to be there (5–7 years).' 'Whenever he's told to do anything he will deliberately do something quite different (6½ years).' 'When I ask him to do something he completely ignores me (7 years).' 'She is asked to tidy her part of the bookshelves and when we go to look later on we find she hasn't touched it (10 years).'

That is the kind of report that we hear from nursery workers and assistants in schools. Parents can give numberless examples, too. This kind of behaviour on the part of children can be a nuisance. It makes life more difficult for adults who are responsible for the practical planning and smooth running of life and work for children, but there are two sides to the matter. Obedience is natural to young children — they expect to obey but on the other hand they are developing independence and they want to exercise it. We like them to show initiative and resource — we should be alarmed if they never asserted themselves or did things on their own or had their own opinions. It is only when we get muddled about when obedience is necessary and how we should demand it that trouble arises.

Children can be left free to choose for themselves in a good many matters even when they are quite young — about, for instance, what toys to take to bed; whether to play in or out of doors when the weather is fine; who to have at a birthday party; where to go for a walk or expedition. The choice is wide in nursery school and infant school and it widens as they grow older, so that by adolescence they are making most of their own decisions. But parents, teachers and other adults must make the decisions that involve health, safety and education for children too immature and inexperienced to plan their own lives, and they will require these decisions to be observed.

We should make as few rules as possible and they should be reasonable ones. We should be quite sure that the children all know what the rules are and understand them. Then we should be consistent about them.

We ourselves should be reliable, too. The children must be able to trust us, to know that we keep our promises to them and they must be able to rely on the information we give them.

The way in which we ask a child to do what we want makes all the difference between obedience and disaster. We should take for granted he will do as we ask and we should make the request clearly and simply. This is particularly true for the very young child who is still struggling with language. It is best to ask him to do one thing at a time. We should be quite sure that he hears and understands what we say. Not only are words new and puzzling but the child's interpretation of our words may be different from ours because his experience is limited. It is a mistake to say, 'Would you like to do so-and-so?' if we intend him to do it because if he says 'No' we cannot insist unless we are dishonest.

If he is busy and we want him to do something else, like come to dinner or go to bed, we should be courteous and sensible enough to warn him a few minutes ahead so that he is prepared for the interruption or the end of his play. He will otherwise quite rightly resent our swooping down to carry him off.

We should try to be as positive in our demands as we can — that is, it is better to ask him to do something than not to do the opposite, for example, 'Please play only on the path and the lawn', not 'Don't play on the bank and the flower beds.' But if we have to forbid something it is no use expecting him to remember about it next day or the next time he has the opportunity to do it; a pleasant reminder is necessary: 'Remember Mrs Jones doesn't like you to climb on her fence.' We must also be ready to give him an honest reason if he asks for it. Our requests should never descend to nagging. If a definite request is not obeyed within a reasonable time we should do something about it and not go on repeating it. If we have to nag then either our request is not essential or we have not made it sensibly. It is very silly to insist on something we cannot enforce and it is just as silly to make threats we cannot carry out.

As the child grows older and understands more about the way things work he takes more responsibility in his group — family or school — and we can discuss rules and methods of organisation with him. He will help to make some of the community regulations and then he will be eager to see that they are kept by everyone. He will have scant respect for a bossy or self-important adult and will demand reasonable explanations of prohibition and orders.

Why does he disobey?

Adults sometimes say of children of any age 'But why won't he obey?' The answer varies with the child's age and understanding and, of course, with the circumstances and with the adult's personality. Some of the reasons may be these:

1. We may be requiring obedience for its own sake instead of as a practical, immediate step towards helping the child to understand the situation. Obedience for its own sake has no real value.
2. The child may not understand what we want him to do; we may have spoken too fast or used unfamiliar words, or his idea of what we have said is not what we meant. A young child has no idea of time. He doesn't understand past and future or how time passes, or how long it takes to do something, or what 'now' and 'at once' mean. He does not mean to disobey but is confused.
3. The child may be thinking of something else or be totally absorbed in his play and has not taken in what we have said. Or he may be living through a fantasy or a make-believe situation at that moment and can't bear to have it interrupted.
4. His urge to explore and investigate may be so strong that he simply disregards us when we say 'No'. This is why parents find children persistently 'fiddling with the knobs' on television sets or turning the taps on cookers when they have expressly forbidden these things. It is a good thing to show him how to turn the television knobs correctly and then when it is time for him to watch a programme to let him switch it on himself.

At all ages most children find some activities or places irresistible. For instance, a housemother says of an eight-year-old boy 'We told him not to slide down the banisters because the newel post was loose and we thought it was dangerous, but he simply went on doing it'; and a classroom assistant says, 'I told the children not to cook today because the stores had not come and we had no margarine or eggs left. But a little while later I found two six-year-olds making a cake. They had used flour, a whole drum of ground ginger, half a packet of chocolate powder and some syrup.' We understand this kind of thing so well because we ourselves often do things we can't resist although it is not wise to do them.

5. A child may refuse to do what he is asked to do because of some anxiety he cannot express or he may have some obsession about it which makes him refuse. The four-year-old mentioned earlier, who stood on the climbing frame and refused to go in to dinner at the nursery school, had some kind of anxiety about eating with a number of other children. This continued when she went to the infant school: nothing would persuade her to eat with the others although at home she was a normal eater enjoying her food and never fussing. This kind of refusal to do what we want must be treated with sympathy and the issue should never be forced. We may need specialist help in such cases or they may solve themselves in time.

6. The child may simply not want to do what we ask and he feels he has the right to say so. We can respect this even if we have to insist. As he gets older we can explain our reasons in more detail, but the reasons must be good ones before we can expect him to accept them.

7. The request may have been made in an abrupt or overbearing manner which makes the child resist. We would probably make the same response to such an order.

8. Of course the child may be deliberately defying the adult — trying out his own independence or expressing rebellion or seeing what the limits of the adult's patience are. The young child may do this actively by saying 'Shan't', or by deliberately doing what has been forbidden. The older child may ignore an adult, or pretend he has not heard.

Sometimes a child who is not sure of being loved or who feels guilty about his own hostile feelings towards an adult will be disobedient on purpose to test the extent of the punishment he will be given — he wants to know how terrible the adult's anger can be, then he will feel safer because he knows the worst. This child needs special care and understanding.

What do we do?

To recognise these reasons for disobedience may help us to understand the situation, but there is still the problem of dealing with it. What should we do when children flatly disobey? First of all we must make sure we are clear about what we are asking him to do.

Sometimes for all our care the trouble is that we are still a little muddled about our reasons for wanting something done, or we are astray in the importance we put on things. I once watched an incident in an Australian nursery school which illustrates what I mean. An intelligent little boy was building with blocks on the floor in front of the shelves on which the blocks were stored. He stopped building and began to run outside. A young nursery assistant stopped him and said, 'Jerry, you haven't put the blocks away. Please put them back on the shelves.' He said 'Why?' and she answered, 'Because then the other children can find them if they want them.' He replied 'They can find them here just as well', which was quite true. The assistant changed her ground and said, 'They are untidy. The room looks nicer when it is tidy.' He said, 'It's nice like this', and ran outside. In this case the nursery assistant failed to get the boy's cooperation because she was not honest with him. She should have taken his question 'Why?' seriously and given him the correct answer which was that space in that part of the playroom was limited. She should have said, 'Because when the blocks are all over the floor there isn't much room for the children to do other things. When they are on the shelves there is more space.' He would have accepted that.

In situations of this kind some nursery assistants say 'Because that's what we always do in our nursery', but this is an evasion. The intelligent child knows quite well that that is 'what we always do'. What he wants to know is why we do it.

Although it is important to be orderly, and a chaotic room where nothing can be found does not encourage play, our ideas of what looks 'nice' or tidy are not the same as the children's. They don't see things in the same way as we do who are responsible for the whole arrangement and we must beware of imposing rules for the children which are only designed to give us satisfaction.

We often have to make quick decisions when we are faced with a refusal to cooperate. If an assistant says to a child, 'If you have finished with these tools will you hang them up, please?' and he, on the point of running out to join a group doing something interesting outside, says 'No', what does she do? She may:

1. Let him go, and put away the tools herself. Knowing the particular child and his problems, she may decide that this is the

right thing to do; or she may be unsure of herself and not know what else to do.

2. Refuse to let him go until the job is done. This may lead to a tantrum in which both are exhausted by the time the job is over; or the child may do as she wants and lose the joy of a new experience with his group of friends; or he may persist in his refusal so that the tools are not put away and her authority is undermined.

3. Say: 'I'll help you. We'll do it quickly and then you can go out'. He will have made the gesture and can still have his fun.

4. Say: 'Run out now and you can put them away when you come in for dinner,' in which case his opposition will have time to evaporate. She will probably have to remind him when he comes in, but pleasantly, confident that he will do it.

When a child refuses to keep a sensible rule and we decide to take positive steps about it we must remember that these steps are only justified if they are constructive, that is, if they help the child to understand why the rule is sensible, and what are the effects of disobedience. They should never be in the nature of revenge by us on the child. We can refuse to let him use the tools or bricks for a few days if he won't put them away; we can remove him from the room if he persists in being noisy or destructive; we can give him a table and chair by himself if he persists in behaving badly at the dinner-table; we can confiscate a hammer if he persists in hitting people or smashing things with it. But we must explain why we do these things and do them without losing our temper. Children who are naturally loving and reasonable respond fairly quickly to this kind of logical treatment.

I do not think we should try to force children to help us or other children. Nursery school children usually enjoy helping with things like setting tables but during the infant school years children prefer to do things because they have to be done rather than because it is helpful to the grown-ups to do them. This means that they often refuse requests to help or go away pretending not to hear; on the other hand we may find on another occasion that they have done the job without being asked. During the junior school years group life is so important to children that adults' rules are often ignored or forgotten because they don't seem important. The children now depend much less on adults (although not as little as they would like to believe) and they like to show this by truculence or insolence or dumb defiance. This can be very hard to deal with but fundamentally most children are reasonable or respond to a reasonable approach. We may be making the mistake of forgetting they are no longer babies and are now old enough to be treated as colleagues.

There still remains the problem of the child who is consistently defiant and wilful despite reasonable demands and encouragement to cooperate. He is usually a deeply unhappy child without real friends among the other children. He may need skilful help beyond what parents, teachers and assistants can give him and the parents and teacher may decide to ask the advice of the schools' psychologist.

Finally, we should know when to ignore disobedience. We all have days when everything goes wrong, when we are tired or out of sorts or unhappy, so we can recognise when the children feel like this and we can then show a blind eye, a deaf ear and an extra comforting touch.

Children who need reassurance

All children need to feel loved and wanted and fortunately most of them do feel this. At times they need extra reassurance and these are usually times when they meet unfamiliar situations, big or small. The staff of day nurseries, playgroups and nursery schools understand that children need reassurance from them for some time after they first come. For instance, an assistant in a nursery school expects behaviour from a new child which shows this need — clinging, shyness, timidity, crying even screaming — and she readily gives extra gentleness and attention to him until he begins to gain confidence and to take part in the nursery activities. She takes time to talk to the new child, to make sure he understands which is his peg in the cloakroom and how to find the lavatory. She shows him where things are kept and asks him to help her with little tasks until he finds his way about the strange place. She is prepared to take him on her lap at dinner-time if it proves to be too difficult for him to face eating at a table with strange children, and she may do the same at rest time, or she may keep him close beside her and talk quietly to him about his mother who will soon be coming to take him home. But she expects that within a few weeks he will no longer need so much special care.

Similarly, the classroom helper in an infant school expects new five-year-olds to need special care and reassurance and the teacher has almost certainly planned the routine of the first weeks of term to allow time for this.

Foster parents and the staff of residential Homes are faced with a much bigger problem and they know they are dealing with deeply troubled and anxious children. Their training helps them to understand the kind of behaviour which betrays the fear and sense of loss these children feel and they are not worried by it though they may find it moving.

There are, however, some children in most normal groups who show the need for constant reassurance by the adults and their behaviour does sometimes worry or disturb teachers and assistants. These children have been in nursery or school long enough to be familiar with the routine and are experienced enough for us to expect them to be independent as long as nothing unexpected or alarming happens, but they do not show the strength of independence we expect and they demand constant attention.

Their ways of doing this may vary considerably and these are some of the remarks we hear from assistants about these children: 'He whines all day long'; 'she clamours at me all the time to look at her drawing (or modelling or sewing)'; 'he cries over the least little thing'; 'he will keep arguing, he always has to go one better and have the last word'; 'she keeps on saying "It's not fair" all the time'; 'she clings to me and won't let me get on with my work'; 'he won't wait till it's his turn, he must have immediate attention'; 'she whimpers in a high-pitched tone if I don't attend to her the moment she asks'; 'she shows great affection and loves to put her arms round my neck and whisper to me but if I show any special attention to another child she sulks'; 'he tugs at my arm to attract my attention so often that I can hardly speak calmly'; 'he tells me about his father's job and his mother's washing-up machine and things like that and none of it's true'; 'he's a terrible show-off'; 'she always has to be the centre of attention and as soon as we [adults] begin a conversation she must break in and interrupt'; 'if no one is taking any notice of her she talks very loudly until we have to ask her to stop'; 'if she thinks she's left out of anything she feels sick or has a headache'; 'he keeps on asking the same questions over and over until I get really cross'; 'she wants to help me all the time'; 'he isn't very popular but he is always giving the children comics or sweets.'

These remarks were made about children of nursery, infant and junior school ages. Children who behave in these ways show that they feel unsure of themselves. How deeply each child feels this it may be impossible for us to know. He may grow stronger quite quickly; the behaviour which irritates us may belong to the stage of development he is now in and may disappear as he matures. On the other hand he may feel neglected, snubbed or ignored. He may be haunted by some anxiety or fear we cannot know about. He may be driven almost beyond bearing by feelings of helplessness, weakness or ignorance. He may be resentful or jealous of brothers and sisters and cannot show that he is for fear of reprisal or rejection. He may believe he is not loved as much as the other children in his family. This may really be so or he may feel it to be so; in either case the hurt is there. The cause may lie beyond our power to remedy and we can only offer what help we can by trying to build up the child's self confidence. This may take patience, time and care, and the teacher will want to know the parents' views on the child's behaviour so that she can plan with her assistant how best to treat the child.

Whining

Let us consider the whiner. Whining is basically a call for help and usually comes from a child who has not been treated reasonably or consistently so that he is bewildered about what adults really require of him. Whining children often have loving parents who have not considered clearly what standards of behaviour they will set for their children and so are muddled themselves about what to allow and what to forbid. Their children are therefore also muddled and because sometimes they are indulgently allowed to behave in ways which at other times are unaccountably forbidden they are unsure of their approach to all adults. The constantly whining child is asking for reassurance and we only make matters worse for him if we let him see that we are irritated. He needs clear demands and a reasonable approach in all we ask him to do. We may have to help him by explaining in a friendly way that we do not like to be asked for something in that particular tone, that we are ready to help him and that we want him to do so-and-so. Above all we must be consistent in our treatment of him and we must never allow him to wear us down and give in to his demands just because we can't bear his whining any longer.

A child who has been normally reasonable but who becomes a whiner may be revealing another problem. He may be bored. This is unlikely in a good nursery school or a busy modern infant school but it is worth our while to check that the occupations available to him are appropriate to his age or, more important, to his ability. He may have outstripped the rest of his group and there is not enough material for him to go on as fast as he wants to do. On the other hand he may be falling behind his group and feels left out.

The child who only occasionally whines is probably tired or not well. He may be incubating a cold or he may have a rising temperature or just feel vaguely off colour. In any case his whining is a sign to us that he needs attention, help and sympathy.

Boasting and showing-off

Some adults find boasting and showing-off in children tiresome but at some ages it is so natural for them to do it that we should expect it and not let it irritate us any more than the baby wetting his napkin does.

When a baby first discovers that what he does makes his parents laugh he does it over and over and they all have much fun. When the baby grows a little and gets about on his own to explore the world he is so absorbed in this that, as long as he has freedom to make his discoveries, he plays these games less often. He now demands more serious cooperation from his parents. If he feels neglected or left out or bored he may try to recapture the attention he had as a baby by performing the antics that amused his parents then and he is usually bewildered and grieved to find they no longer think he is funny.

By the time he is about four and a half he is becoming sure of himself as a person and of his skill and power. He is quite naturally and healthily self-centred and self-absorbed at this stage and for the next few years, and so towards the end of the nursery school period and through most of the infant school years we may find him telling us how strong and clever he is, how high he can jump, how fast he can ride, what tremendous feats he has performed and will perform and so on. We can say 'Splendid! Show me how you do it'; or, if he threatens us, as he sometimes does ('I'll ride into you and knock you down and ride right over you!') we can say 'Right! On you come and we'll see what happens' and turn it into a romp. Of course, because he is loving and generous as well, he will often say 'I'll buy a lorry-load of ice-cream and give it to you!'

A different reason for what adults sometimes call showing-off or demanding attention is that the child has suddenly found the key to a skill such as reading or writing or sewing and is intoxicated (as we would be ourselves) with the excitement of it. He wants to show us all the time what he can do, 'Hear me read this'; 'Look, I've got down to here now'; 'Watch me do this'; often accompanied by tugs at the arm or pulls at the dress. We must not snub him now – this is a turning point in his life; this is when he needs our praise and admiration and encouragement to go on. If we can recognise the genuine joy and triumph and respond to it it does not matter if for a few days we give this child more attention than we give to the others.

It is when showing-off or boasting seems to be a pointless habit that we see that something has gone wrong. We feel that the child is insecure for some reason and needs our constant reassurance. It may be an attempt to overcome shyness or self-consciousness. Quite often it is the rather plain, insignificant child who shows off because he feels plain and dull. It may be that he distrusts adults because his parents don't tell him the truth or they make him feel that they have lost interest in him.

In cases like this we need to build up the child's confidence in every way we can. We may show him new ways of doing things — how to hold the saw more efficiently; how to grasp the scissors more firmly; how to throw a ball straight. Or we can introduce him (or her) to new skills altogether — painting on a new kind of paper with different brushes or with a new kind of paint; how to sew a new kind of seam to make a doll's dress stronger (a fresh piece of pretty material helps, too); a new way to cook biscuits; how to use screws instead of nails. We can give him small but definite responsibilities within his capacity and we can try to make him legitimately the centre of attention every now and again by finding out if he has any special interest and asking him to tell the group about it. He may have an auntie in South America or New Zealand whose letters have beautiful stamps on them or who sometimes sends interesting post-cards; or his father may breed canaries or fish; or his big brother may play football for a local club or secondary school; or his mother may have won a prize for her knitting or cake-making; or he himself may keep mice or collect matchboxes.

Older children sometimes behave in rather silly ways when they are embarrassed or don't know what is expected of them in a new situation. This can usually be ignored or eased by a matter-of-fact comment.

Groups of children sometimes 'go silly' and posture and grimace and say wilder and wilder things. This may happen when visitors come into the nursery or classroom. It may also be a sign that for some reason they have not been physically active enough — perhaps bad weather has kept them indoors in a confined space for longer than usual. Some on-the-spot jumping and whirling and bending to music or singing for fun with vigorous actions may remedy the silliness without our having to comment on it.

Nursery school teachers and assistants often find that a child shows off or acts in a silly way when his mother comes to take him home or brings him in the morning. It is when both adults are in the room together that it happens. The child seems not able to cope with both adults at once and it may be more marked in cases where what the parents expect of the child is not the same as the behaviour the nursery expects. The child is just confused. This is best ignored, too, but the signal should be noted by both sides and they may be able to meet for some discussions about the child when he is not around.

In any case most boasting and showing-off is a temporary matter: the child will grow out of it and we need only show good humour and common sense about it. In the cases where we believe it to be a symptom of something more serious we must steadily show affection in the form of positive help and guidance in practical matters and be the kind of person the child can learn to trust and rely on.

Lying and stealing

These are kinds of behaviour which cause grown-ups to worry, mostly without cause although some children who lie and steal need reassurance and occasional children need special help.

It is not until most children are well into the junior school period that they become completely truthful in the adult sense or that they develop a factual idea of ownership and property rights. So it is not sensible of us to do more than help young children to disentangle facts and attitudes about these things.

Let us take lying first. The little child up to five or six years at least, is still struggling to work out what is fact and what is fantasy. Fortunately, he has a lively imagination if he is alert and intelligent, and he mixes up what he would like to do, what he intends to do, what he has already done and what he thinks we should like him to do, all together. The three- or four-year-old will emphatically deny having done something we accuse him of doing, even though we can point to the evidence right in front of him. This is not really lying: he doesn't want to have done what makes us angry and he is sure he hasn't done it. This kind of rejection of his wrong-doing is still found in most children up to the second year of the infant school and it is only when, by about six-and-a-half, the child recognises that his mates are sometimes not telling the truth, that it begins to be important to him. He can then become quite strict about it.

We can enjoy the fantastic tales the four- and five-year-olds tell us about their adventures when we know this is a normal phase in their development. We can make sympathetic comments and at the same time gently introduce an element of fact. For instance, if a boy runs in and says, 'I pulled a policeman out of the river and he thanked me!' we can say 'I should think so, he might have drowned if you hadn't been there. Was he very heavy? Did you have to jump in to get him?' Or if a girl says, 'There were two bears in our garden last night!' we can say, 'Good gracious! Were they black bears or brown bears?'

When we give the children plenty of opportunity to do real things well they will pass through this period of fantasy quite normally. If they have little opportunity or encouragement to be active and creative they may prolong the stage of make-believe and fall into the habit of day-dreaming which can be destructive to effort and learning.

Some children exaggerate in order to make an impression on their mates or on the adults, telling tall stories about their fathers' prowess or their family possessions. Usually they soon outgrow this phase. If a child continues doing this for a long time it may be a sign that he feels unsure of himself. In that case he is like the boaster we discussed earlier and should be helped in the same way by the building up of self-confidence. A child of seven or more who lies a good deal is either frightened of punishment or is unhappy and unsettled for some reason. If he is harshly treated at home for doing things his parents don't like he may panic and lie at school when he is questioned about some misdemeanour. The teacher and the parents may be able to discuss the matter of punishment together and ease the situation. If a child with whom we are working lies a great deal although we are sure our treatment of him is fair and affectionate and the parents do not appear to be overstrict or unjust, we may have to suggest asking the advice of specialists in the schools' psychological service.

Needless to say we should always be completely honest with the children we are working with. If they can't trust us to tell them the truth we can't blame them for lying to us.

Now the question of stealing; as I have already said (p. 83) the little child is confused about what ownership is and how to behave when he wants something someone else has. He gradually learns about these things as he becomes aware of owning things himself and sees how we respect his ownership. We don't use his things without asking his permission and we allow him to lend them or not as he wishes. So that he can learn the value of money and goods we should give him pocket money from the time he goes to school and let him spend it as he likes.

When he is young the child believes that what belongs to his family belongs to him. This is why he takes for granted that he can ask his friends in to play in his garden and offer them food from his larder or that he can take an armful of flowers to school from the garden without asking. Parents have to treat this kind of behaviour sympathetically but sensibly. They may have to make some kind of provision about what food he can offer to his mates — mother may put aside a special tin of biscuits and a bottle of milk or squash for him to share. Father may want to be consulted about which flowers he may take to school.

It is most valuable if children in residential Homes know they can share food and other things in this way. If house-parents can let them feel the family goods are partly theirs to give away to friends outside the Home it makes them feel really part of a loving family.

When children make mistakes about ownership we have to show them what to do. Ken went to the supermarket with his mother and when she was unpacking her shopping basket at home he took a tablet of soap out of his pocket and gave it to her. She asked him whether he took it from the shelf in the supermarket and explained about paying for goods in shops. Hand in hand they went back and explained to the cashier and Ken handed over the money for the soap. Children often take home small toys from the nursery school and sensible mothers explain that they belong to all the children and make sure the children hand them back next day.

When a child is excited and enthusiastic about some work he is doing at the nursery or in the infant school he may take anything he needs without asking the owner's permission. This is not stealing although the teacher or assistant may point out that he should have asked before he took it and must give it back if the owner insists. She will then help him find something else as good for the purpose.

There are times when we realise the child's behaviour is verging on stealing as we understand it. If we find a child constantly taking money or food or trinkets we suspect that there is something wrong, especially if we find he is not using the things he takes in his own work or play but is hiding them or giving them away. He may feel he is not loved or wanted or a formerly secure home situation may be changing in a way that frightens him or makes him anxious.

Robert lived with an aunt and uncle in England because his parents were working abroad. He went to a local school but spent his summer holidays abroad with his parents. During the autumn term when Robert was nine years old his aunt began to miss small sums of money from her purse and tins of food from her larder. She took no notice for a while except to arrange for Robert to have more pocket money in case he did not have enough to meet his social needs at school. When the pilfering continued she and her husband began to worry in case Robert was taking things from school as well but there was no complaint of this from the headmaster. Towards the end of the term rumours of a rift between the parents filtered through to the family. It became plain that Robert had sensed something was wrong during the summer holidays. Efforts to save the marriage failed and during the following months Robert's pilfering went on.

His aunt and uncle were careful not to leave money about but other-wise did nothing except try to give Robert support in what ways they could. As soon as his parents' divorce was decided, however, the stealing suddenly ceased. It seems that Robert pilfered because his anxiety about what was going on was too great to be borne with-out comfort. He tried to get this by taking the money and the food and giving it to his school mates. Once he knew exactly what was going to happen he felt less anxious. He was not happy about the break-up of his parents' marriage but at least it was something definite. His school work, which had suffered, picked up again and he was altogether happier and freer.

This kind of stealing should be handled with great care because the child does not know exactly why he is doing it and he is miserable about the whole thing. Fortunately if the adults concerned try to understand the reason for the stealing and remove that, if they can, the child usually stops stealing fairly soon. If the adults are shocked and horrified and punish the child he is not helped but made worse. He will begin to hide his thieving and lie about it as well.

This is not the place to discuss the kind of stealing which is the result of deliberately bad example at home so that it becomes a calculated criminal act. That is a matter for specialists and the class teacher and her assistant will not have the responsibility of dealing with it once they have established its nature.

The quiet child

Some adults say that they are a little worried by shy children who find it hard to join in with others even though they would like to.

An assistant can help a child who is ordinarily nervous and shy of new situations and new people if she has the imagination to see with the child's eyes how it all looks to him. We have already said some-thing about this (see p. 103). The secret is never to rush him in any way but to slow down the pace of life around him, if she can, until he has adjusted his tempo and got things into focus. While this is happening he can stay close to the assistant and follow her about if he wants to. Bit by bit he will be tempted to try things out in the interesting surroundings of nursery, playgroup or classroom. The grown-up's encouragement should be implicit rather than urgent. She can suggest things to do, but casually as she goes about her own business, and she should never thrust ideas at him or take any notice if he doesn't do what she suggests. It may be a long time — some-times many weeks — before a shy child plucks up courage to give and take with the other children but usually in the end he takes his place in the group. He may retreat from time to time but these times will probably become fewer as he gains confidence. He may never be as noisy or vigorous as some of the others but will be able to make his own characteristic contribution to the group.

Sometimes we have a new child who comes from so orderly and careful a home that he is overcome by the strenuous play of the other children and by the wealth of activity in the nursery or class and can do nothing but stand and watch. This child may refuse to paint or play in the sandpit, or take part in any messy activity for a long time. Quite suddenly we may find that he throws off his restraint and becomes the noisiest and dirtiest and most enterprising of all the children, a leader in mischief and ingenuity. More often he remains restricted in his play and needs a good deal of encouragement. If his parents can be introduced to the work of the nursery or school so that they come to approve of all the activities this will help the child a great deal. He will not feel then that he is displeasing them by getting his hands or his clothes grubby.

There is another, rather small, group of quiet children whom we may meet. They are self-contained, observant and usually highly intelligent. They have no objection to any of the usual play in the nursery or classroom but it doesn't greatly interest them. They are usually found in the book corner or building or painting or modelling quietly by themselves. They tend to hold long conversations with adults or with each other and to watch carefully and remark on the behaviour of the other children. It is a mistake to try and force these children to play robustly. They are playing in their own way. All the material is available to them if they want to use it. They are often imaginative but tend to put their fantasies into words rather than to act them out in make-believe play with other children. When they are a little older they will be the ones to write the class play and perhaps take part in the action. They read early and master writing quickly. In the classroom they need a wealth of material to work at. They are seldom leaders of the group, preferring to observe and criticise, but they are quite capable of accepting responsibility. Sometimes they argue with teacher and assistant but usually they accept what they are asked to do and go ahead at their own rapid pace.

The group of quiet children who should worry us are those who are too anxious or too highly controlled to let themselves go and to play vigorously. They may appear to be 'good' children, polite and giving no trouble, but they may in fact be ill children, tensed like coiled springs. What has caused them to grow like this we may not know but we can usually recognise them by the quality of their quietness. There is an unnatural stillness about them; they are often pale and their movements are controlled and careful. They seem to be afraid of knocking things over or of dropping things or spoiling material. Their painting is usually cramped and small. It almost seems as if they are so frightened of being rough and destructive that they hardly dare do anything at all. Occasionally these children have screaming bouts or fits of hysterical crying and if this happens it may give them some temporary relief but they are children who need great care and help. Unfortunately it is specialist help they need and probably the best thing we can do for them is to suggest that they should have it if the parents agree, while at the same time we can make sure they have opportunities to tear, cut, hammer, pound and dig if they will take them. (See also p. 160.)

Nervous habits

High on the list of behaviour in children that adults find difficult is a group of nervous habits such as sniffing, tapping with the fingers or with a ruler, whistling through the teeth, thumb sucking, picking at noses or nails, grimacing, grinding teeth, jumping and hopping, carrying a rag or a particular toy about all the time. These things may be irritating but they are not as a rule dangerous. If we are honest we would make a list of all the little nervous habits we have which might well irritate children! However much they are loved and looked after, children do find life difficult and puzzling and if carrying a rag about or sucking a thumb comforts or helps a child we should be able to ignore it. Our responsibility is to see that his world is rich in opportunities for play and work, to give him our love and support. If we do this then his small nervous habits will in time disappear.

Further reading

Chaloner, Len, *Feeling and Perception in Young Children*, Tavistock, 1963.
Chesters, Gwendolen E., *The Mothering of Young Children*, 2nd edn, Faber, 1956, particularly Chapters 9, 10 and 11.
Isaacs, Susan, *Social Development in Young Children*, Routledge, 1933.
Isaacs, Susan, *Troubles of Children and Parents*, Methuen, 1948.
May, D. E., *Children in the Nursery School*, University of London Press, 1963.
Peters, Jocelyn, *Growing Up World*, Longman, 1966.
Winnicott, D. W., *The Child, the Family and the Outside World*, Penguin: Pelican, 1964, particularly Part Two, 24 and Part Three, 31.

Chapter 6

Feeding children

Food is such a fundamental part of our life it is not surprising that so many emotions are aroused by any mention of it. It is at the centre of most of our social life and is a source of great pleasure as well as anxiety, rivalry and pride.

Mothers spend a lot of time choosing and preparing food for their families and get angry and concerned when it is criticised or not eaten. They worry about feeding their babies and are anxious when children have no appetite or feel sick after eating. Children often use food and eating as weapons against their mothers and mealtimes can become a battleground between children and grown-ups.

Parents know that food is something which children need, that it is necessary to sustain life, to promote healthy growth; at the same time it is something which they enjoy giving their child, it is valuable because it is part of a loving, caring relationship between them and their children. Young children are not interested in the nutritional value of food. They are interested in satisfying their hunger, in the texture, colour and taste of food and, most importantly, in their relationship with the person providing the food. Babies look on food only in terms of this relationship. They do not separate food from being fed.

We realise that unless food is kept clean and made safe by cooking and careful storage it can carry the germs of disease and we also know that unless we give children a good mixed diet they will not grow strong and healthy. Because we know about these things and are not working by chance or magic we feel free to give food generously and lovingly to children and this helps our relationship with them.

Feeding babies

The most intimate feeding relationship is the breast feeding of her baby by the mother. The mother enjoys holding her baby and giving him love in the form of nourishment from her own body. To the baby it means warm bodily contact, a feeling of being safe and sheltered and a stimulating activity that leads to contentment and satisfaction. After the first pangs of hunger are satisfied the baby can also enjoy gentle play in his mother's arms, touching and stroking her breast and face.

If difficulties arise and breast feeding is not possible the mother will try to create the same situation, holding her baby in her arms while he is fed. Babies who are left in prams or cots with a propped-up feed bottle are in a physically dangerous and emotionally deprived situation. A loving, secure environment at feed-time helps to establish the bond between mother and child.

When a nursery nurse feeds someone else's baby she also tries to create a loving situation. She makes food for him as much like his mother's as possible and gives it to him as lovingly as she can in an unhurried, tranquil manner. It is important that, as in the situation with his mother, the baby is not rushed, that he decides the pace at which he will take his food and that he is given time to play and to respond to the person feeding him.

When he is a little older, a new situation arises for the baby when solid food is introduced into his diet. He is growing fast, becoming more active and he needs more protein and energy foods. His digestive juices are capable of dealing with more solid food, his prenatal store of iron needs replenishing and his gums are becoming hard as his teeth push upward so that he begins to enjoy biting instead of sucking. For all these reasons cereals, eggs, vegetables, rusks, and later, meat and fish are gradually added to his feeds. He has to learn to enjoy new tastes and new textures, a new feel to his food.

It is important to add these things slowly and gradually at first so that he accepts them as new forms of affection and does not feel that the old love is being taken away from him. If he has felt secure and happy about his feeding up to now he will readily try the new tastes because he trusts the person who offers them. If he refuses at first he should be given plenty of time and not forced in any way to take his new food. The keynote of introducing mixed feeding is leisureliness with the adult adopting a relaxed manner. If he has taken his fruit juice or cod liver oil from a spoon he will already be used to the feel of a spoon in his mouth and new food can be introduced slowly and gently. Later on he will take milk from a cup quite readily but he may need to be comforted by a bottle for some time afterwards when he is tired or sick or anxious. Even when he is old enough to have meals three times a day -- perhaps at about nine months — he still likes to be fed on mother's or nurse's lap with her arms around him. He enjoys the contact. If the transition from milk five times a day to three solid meals has been accomplished in a leisurely, steady fashion and accepted happily by the baby then he will be ready to take future changes in his life in his stride and will be likely to go out to meet new situations with confidence.

Put briefly like this the change from milk to solid food does not sound difficult. But, as I have said earlier (p. 8) many problems and difficulties can arise at this time because weaning makes big emotional demands on the baby. This book is not the place to go more thoroughly into the matter but the nursery staff in charge of a baby at this stage should be aware of the difficulties and should read further about weaning and its meaning for the baby. Certainly the same nurse should take any one baby through this stage and she should have the knowledgeable support of the rest of the staff. Mothers these days have the advantage of being able to use specially designed kitchen utensils which simplify the preparation of baby's solid food, or they can, if they wish, choose to buy the food from the large selection available in the shops. They do not make such heavy weather of weaning as their grandmothers did.

Feeding toddlers

By the time he is a year old life is full of interest and excitement for the toddler. He is beginning to do things for himself, to express his wishes in positive ways and he is much more active. He wants to reach out to do and to experience all kinds of things by himself. At mealtimes he is now able to sit in a baby chair, usually with a tray and he is happy to try using a spoon to dig into his food. We should try to make quite sure that he is comfortable in his chair, not slipping forward and that he feels secure and happy. If the baby chair is placed on an adult chair so that the baby is at the same eye level height as his mother or nurse, particular care should be taken that he is not likely to try to climb out and fall. Some people like to use a harness of some kind to prevent accidents, making sure that it is tight enough to stop him slipping but loose enough to let him move his shoulders and arms freely. Even with a harness accidents can still happen if the baby is left unattended. Many mothers prefer to leave the baby chair at ground level, sitting on a low stool to help him feed himself so that he can easily see his mother's face. This avoids the need for any harness and gives the baby greater freedom.

His mother or nurse will need a spoon as well because most of the food he actually eats will be put into his mouth by her. There is often a good deal of mess at this stage – food on the baby's face, over the tray and on the floor. He is still not at all accurate in controlling his arms and getting food from his plate to his mouth, but he urgently wants to try. As long as we know that feeding at this stage takes a long time and is likely to be messy we will prepare for it and not fuss. His clothes need to be covered by a large bib of the apron type and it is useful to put a square of plastic or a newspaper under his chair to save washing the floor. In a day nursery where there are a number of babies at this stage of development the staff are prepared for the practical problems mealtimes involve. A mother alone with her one-year-old has time to remember that he needs encouragement in his efforts to manage his food by himself and to give him her patience and help. It is not so easy in a nursery for us to give each child these things when the staff are shorthanded and a great many practical things have to be done at once.

Let us look at some of the factors involved. On the one hand the meal has to be ready at a certain time and should not be kept heated up for long. The babies' hands and faces must be washed and most nurseries like to pot them first as well to save interruptions during the meal. This can't be done all at the same moment for all the babies. On the other hand the babies, anxious to crawl actively about and to practise pulling themselves up — after all the main business of their lives at this stage — should not be left in their chairs for too long and left with nothing to do until everybody is ready. Somehow these conflicting factors have to be resolved in the best way for the babies. It may be better for a baby to sit a little longer than is comfortable in a chair, chewing a rusk, and then to be fed happily rather than to sit for a shorter time and be fed by a rushed and overworked nurse with no time to talk and laugh with him about it all. Ideally each baby would be fed as soon as he is ready.

As long as we remember that babies of this age are essentially active, that they are trying to be independent about handling their food, that this is an important step in their growing up and that they need encouragement from us, we shall not go too far wrong. We should adjust any routine that becomes too rigid, we may have to rearrange staff duties or abandon a potting session but once the real values are recognised it should be possible to resolve any problem. It helps to have all the arrangements for serving the food and clearing up as simple as possible and to make things easy for the babies to manage by having spoons with thick straight handles, unbreakable plates that don't slide about and that have straight sides to help the spooning-up movements, and mugs with wide bases and big handles.

Six months later the baby may make a good deal more fuss about having his work interrupted for mealtimes. He will now be walking and exploring freely and this is much more interesting to him than eating. He often does not associate a growing feeling of discomfort with the need for food and resents being bothered to come and wash and sit in his chair. Sometimes he needs firm treatment — to be taken for a few minutes on his nurse's lap and have several spoonfuls of food given to him before he is put into his chair. He finds the food satisfying and comforting and is prepared to give up moving about until he has finished it. By now he can feed himself fairly competently but he still needs a steady chair and practical utensils, and he wants to get down and back to work promptly.

Mealtimes for young children

Meals are more than eating: they are social occasions, an important part of the civilisation in which the child is developing. In his home a child usually has meals sitting at the table with the rest of the family from the time he is about two. Here, without much direct teaching, he learns a great deal about mealtimes by watching and listening. He learns how to use his tools — knives, forks, spoons, cups — and which are the approved methods of eating. He learns how adults behave at the table and what are their attitudes to food and to each other.

There is no doubt that it is important that adults in nurseries and infant schools should share mealtimes with young children. This can be a sacrifice of comfort and relaxation on the part of the staff members but the value to the children is inestimable. Mealtimes are times when we most clearly show that we accept inhibitions to 'natural' desires and impulses in order to live in a 'civilised' way. Children need to know that all adults, not only their own parents, accept these inhibitions. They learn that adults don't snatch or throw food but wait to be served and pass things to each other. They talk pleasantly and happily during meals but they don't shout or quarrel or behave noisily. They use tools for eating and not their hands with certain exceptions. The children discover that there are many different kinds of food, served in different ways and that adults eat it and don't play with it or throw it about. They see that it is possible to eat quietly and in a relaxed manner and yet enjoy food and the company of one's table companions. It is almost never necessary to teach young children 'manners'. In any case, any teaching is probably best done during a home-play session rather than at the table. Children do need to be shown how to hold and use knives and forks but otherwise they learn how to behave by observing and copying. The more unselfconscious the adults are during mealtimes, the more naturally the children absorb the desired behaviour.

Like everything else that sensible adults do with children the effortless appearance of their management of mealtimes is based on careful planning and a knowledge of the children's needs. Perhaps we can sum up these needs in this way:

1. Children need nourishing meals which are served attractively but without fuss.
2. They need mealtimes which are happy and orderly with food served in surroundings as pleasant as we can make them.
3. They enjoy doing a good deal of the helping and serving themselves and the mealtime should be so planned that this is possible.
4. They should be comfortable and relaxed, so they should go to the lavatory and wash their hands before meals, but once they are ready they should not be kept waiting long for their food. They should have chairs and tables which allow them to sit comfortably.
5. They need adult companionship and should feel free to talk to each other and to the adults. The general atmosphere at mealtimes should be casual without being careless. We sometimes become too solemn about meals.

In a nursery school, because of the ratio of staff to children it should be possible for the meals to be served at a leisurely pace and in an intimate atmosphere. Each nursery school has it own plan for serving dinner. The head teacher takes into consideration the plan of the building, the facilities available to the domestic staff and the needs of the children. Some teachers like to have a table or trolley from which all helpings are served by an adult and taken to the tables by children; others prefer an adult at each table to serve for eight or ten children; others have smaller groups of children as families with one of the children, in turn, serving helpings for the others. Others again choose a modification of the cafeteria system. There are many varieties of these arrangements but all give opportunities for the children to help with preparing the room, setting tables, serving others and clearing away. This is sensible because it not only gives the children an opportunity to be helpful and independent but also gives them a chance to practise skills of carrying and pouring and gives them a chance to be active between courses. It also gives them the opportunity to make decisions and judgements in a real practical situation. There are bound to be spills and accidents and wise adults keep mops and cloths nearby to wipe up without fuss.

Meals in the primary school will be rather different from those at home or in the nursery. They may not be so leisurely or intimate because of the larger number of children to be catered for and the smaller number of adults to supervise and help the children. In most schools, although they are not obliged to do so, teachers and class-room assistants opt to eat their mid-day meal with the children and endeavour to make the mealtimes as pleasant, relaxed and socially worthwhile occasions as they are in the nursery school. If a school is fortunate enough to have an area specially set aside for dining purposes, efforts are made to make the room as attractive as possible with children helping to write out the daily menus and brightening the tables with flowers or table decorations which they have made themselves.

As in the nursery, meals may be served in a number of ways, with children either being served or serving each other at the table or being served at a counter in cafeteria style. Because of the rising cost of school meals a large number of children bring packed sandwich lunches to eat at school. Many mothers feel that they can cater for their children's personal likes and dislikes by providing a packed lunch for the child to eat at mid-day and provide a cooked meal for the family to share together in the evening. If mother is sensible and ensures that there is plenty of variety in the packed lunch, with sufficient protein, fruit and not too much carbohydrate there is no reason why the meal should not be just as nourishing as a cooked dinner. On cold days children like to bring warm soup in vacuum flasks of the unbreakable variety which are on the market at present. The children are provided with plates, knives, forks and spoons if required and drinking beakers and jugs of water are placed on the tables. They are encouraged to eat their meals in a civilised way, not forgetting normal table manners.

The question of how dinner tables are set depends on the re-sources available in the school, a consideration of priorities and the preferences of members of staff. Some nursery school teachers, for instance, like to have tablecloths, bowls of flowers and china dishes. These things are sometimes desirable and help to create a pleasant atmosphere if they are used without causing strain or excessive effort but in some cases the staff may decide that they pay too high a price for them in energy which might better be spent on other things. Tablecloths are only attractive if they are clean and fresh, and china is only useful if its breaking can be accepted with serenity. Grubby and creased tablecloths are of no value and if having fresh ones every day becomes a burden, or if keeping watch on china plates and glass tumblers lest they be dropped or overturned makes the adults nervous and irritable, then they are better abandoned in favour of more practical if less gracious furnishings. Tables can have modern surfaces which are attractive and easily cleaned and plates, jugs and cups can be unbreakable as well as pretty. The children can still put bowls of flowers on the tables and set the places carefully and they will not be greatly distressed if they spill or drop things because the table is easily wiped clean and the adults are not perturbed. Tablecloths and china dishes can perhaps be kept for special occasions like birthdays or Christmas parties.

The same principle of weighing priorities applies for infant and junior school mealtimes. The children are older and less likely to spill and drop dishes but the room is often crowded and care must be taken to make the surroundings pleasant. There are many different ways of making tables attractive and so of encouraging the children to enjoy eating together and to behave well, and the adults responsible make their decisions after considering all the factors involved. The kitchen staff, ancillary workers, assistants and teachers are all involved in these decisions.

Adults at the tables with young children set the pace of the meal and the pattern of eating habits. If a child does not eat his food it is best to take little notice and to remember that after all a child is an individual with personal likes and dislikes. His plate can be removed without any fuss. If the child is ill he will show other symptoms and if he is not ill there is no point in drawing attention to his not eating. If he is showing off this may be exactly what he wants. If he is unhappy or anxious no amount of nagging or coaxing to eat will make him feel better: he needs comfort and reassurance in some form and this may be best given just by letting him sit beside the grown-up during the meal and then in some more positive way later. Not eating is a habit which usually resolves itself in time. If it is the symptom of some deepseated trouble this will have to be tackled by specialists. In any case the table is the wrong place to deal with it.

The adult should remember, in a multi-racial society, that some children do not eat certain foods for religious reasons and should try to save the child embarrassment in this situation. Other children may have allergies to certain foods; for example a number of children are allergic to wheat products. Staff should be aware of this and make sure that these children are offered an alternative food.

Mealtimes with large numbers of children are busy times for those in charge and there is always the temptation for adults to do things themselves which should be done by the children. It is quicker and more efficient for adults to clear tables and collect plates and load trolleys but to do these things is to rob the children of opportunities to learn and to grow up.

Snacks

Leaders of playgroups or teachers in part-time nursery schools where there is one group of children in the morning and another in the afternoon do not have a midday meal to organise but usually serve milk or fruit juice and perhaps a biscuit or piece of apple at some time during the session. Whether to serve this refreshment formally or casually is sometimes a problem. Some leaders argue that the children should leave their play for a little while and sit quietly having their milk together in an orderly manner because, since there is no dinner, this is the only opportunity they have to eat together and this is a valuable social experience. Others say, 'There is so little time to play and the children are so engrossed it seems wrong to interrupt them.' In this case they usually set out milk or juice and biscuits on a table about midway through the session. An adult sits nearby and each child, when he is ready, comes to the table and pours his milk or juice into his mug. He may drink it standing and go straight back to his play or he may sit and talk to the grown-up while he has his snack.

A few playgroups and part-time nursery schools serve a light lunch at midday. This may be soup and a salad sandwich, or wholemeal bread and butter and cheese with an apple and milk or some other snack carefully planned to be nourishing and yet conveniently served. In this case the children sit together with an adult to eat it but the service may be cafeteria style or carried out in a more formal manner with children taking turns as waiters and servers.

In any case no one arrangement is suitable for all groups. Each group leader and her staff must decide what is best in their circumstances, remembering that unless a balance is kept between what is valuable for the children and what is sensible for the adults the children suffer in the end. The real interests of children are not served by tired and harassed adults. A sound compromise between what is ideal and what is practical in the circumstances is necessary in each situation. Adults who truly care for children will find out what they need and then set about giving these things to them as sensibly as possible.

Further reading

British Association of Early Childhood Education (pamphlets), (a) *Feeding Young Children*, B.A.E.C.E.; (b) *Mealtimes*, B.A.E.C.E. (Oxford Branch).

Clark, F. de Gros, *A.B.C. of Food and Child Feeding*, National Society of Children's Nurseries.

Clift, P., *Aims, Role and Deployment of Staff in the Nursery*, N.F.G.R., 1980.
Sylva, K. D., Roy, C. and Painter, M., *Childwatching at Playgroup and Nursery School*, Grant McIntyre, 1980.
Winnicott, D. W., *The Child and the Family*, Part I, No. 4 and No. 12, Tavistock, 1957.

Chapter 7

The role of the adult I

What adults do

Young children are entirely dependent on adults for their survival
and care. In most cases each child is looked after by his parents, but
they in turn are sustained and supported by the society of which
they are members. Gradually other adults take over some of the
responsibilities of caring for the child — relatives, neighbours, nurses,
doctors, playgroup leaders, teachers; and every adult the young child
encounters, however casually, affects him by reinforcing or under-
mining his grasp of the real world and his confidence in people. As
he grows the child depends less and less on adults and begins to
order his own life but he cannot altogether escape from his history —
the influence that he and his environment had on each other in his
early years, and the most powerful part of that environment was the
adults who surrounded him then.

It is worth our while to try to set down some of the things that
we do as the responsible adults in the early life of our children.

Making relationships First we make a relationship with each child
with whom we have contact. We cannot avoid doing this. We could
say that the adults in a child's life are something like a frame for him
to climb on, brace himself against, stretch and balance on, attack,
use for make-believe and finally grow out of and reject. The result of
his use of this frame is always with him just as his body is always
influenced by his use of a climbing-frame in his play. His parents give
the fundamental shape of such a framework but each adult the child
knows adds a rung or a new dimension to it.

The relationship between adults and children which is most
helpful to the children is one of love, trust and acceptance; one in
which each knows and expresses the value of the other and can
accept puzzling or trying behaviour in the other without resentment.
This kind of relationship is not based on sentimentality but on love

and honesty. Sentimental adults are often condescending, untruthful and evasive towards children. Loving someone means self-discipline and effort to understand him, and sentimental people are unwilling to make this effort. When we are living and working with children we haven't time to think out what to do at every moment, we behave spontaneously, and this is why our fundamental attitude towards children is important. We make many mistakes but if our basic attitude is one of love and honesty these mistakes are not dangerous.

Providing and planning We provide and plan for our children. We make a warm and interesting place for them to live in; we provide shelter, food, companionship, material for play and work and time to use it.

Setting standards Adults set standards and patterns in skills and in social relationships. Most of this we do unconsciously. Our standards are implicit in our behaviour, in our reaction to situations as they arise, in our attitudes towards other people, in the tones of our voice and in the way we tackle our work. But sometimes we have to be more explicit and then we teach skills and explain why we behave as we do.

Preventing dangers We try to foresee and prevent dangers and distractions for our children. We keep out of their way such adult tools as might hurt them; we guard their health by keeping their surroundings clean, by teaching them to wash themselves, by cooking their food sensibly, by seeing that they change wet shoes and do not fall into unguarded fires or suck poisonous paint; we make sure that play and physical education apparatus is safe and in good order; we supervise games and expeditions; and we cooperate with the community in taking advantage of public health and school medical services. We also try to foresee and prevent some of the tiresome or harmful situations which can arise from their own behaviour and that of their fellows. Of course young children have to quarrel and be rivals as well as to take turns and be helpful if they are to grow up but if we know them well we know when tempers or frustration or aggression can be unnecessarily hurtful and if we can prevent it we will.

Setting bounds Another thing we do is to set bounds. The physical bounds are obvious, there are walls, doors and a fence. The other bounds are concerned with behaviour. As sensible adults, working with any group of children, we will agree together about what rules of behaviour we consider necessary. These will be as few as possible and will be reasonable and clear but we will be consistent about observing them. Young children need adults to set bounds of this kind because it makes them feel safe and they are free to use their energy in working and learning. If they had no rules they would waste energy in anxiety and confusion. If on the other hand the rules are too many or too rigid the children waste time and energy rebelling against them or trying to obey them.

Another way in which we set bounds is to act as arbiters. Young children often need adults to settle their quarrels or to settle disputes over play material.

Stimulation and encouragement   Adults stimulate and encourage children. We encourage the child to develop a lively curiosity about the world around him, and within the bounds of safety, to explore it. We make the best choice that we can in provision of play materials and experiences that will encourage the child to use his imagination, to come to terms with his emotions and learn to handle them, to practise using his body and his senses and to lay the foundations of language skills. It is our responsibility to ensure that there is no need for a child to feel bored and that no child feels discouraged for too long. Praise and encouragement are necessary and helpful but they must be genuine and objective as well as affectionate. Sensible children rightly ignore indiscriminate or insincere praise. Encouragement can be by deed or by word in the form of attention or help, the giving of extra material or the careful answering of questions.

It is obvious that a great deal of our work with children can be called background work — in fact, perhaps our biggest job of all is to form a steady, reliable background for their lives. Of much of this planning and providing the young child is unaware. All parents know that their care for their children is partly remote and partly deeply personal. The young baby comforted and fed by his mother knows nothing of the work of his father which supports and sustains his mother and makes her care of him possible. In all work with children these two roles are played, sometimes both at once by each adult, sometimes separately by different members of a team. As children grow older they become aware gradually that the adults are caring for them by planning and working at times when they are not physically present or directly in touch with them.

The family

In this country it is generally accepted that the best place for a child to grow up is in his own home within his family circle: mother and father, sisters and brothers, with grandparents, aunts, uncles and cousins not too far away. However, studies over the last 20 years give us a picture of family structure and family life which is rather different. The raised status of women, advances in technology within the home, increased mobility, the blurring of conjugal roles, easier divorce, the raised level of education and expectations are some of the factors which have brought about changes in the family.

Modern families, the family of husband, wife and children, have a high degree of mobility. People change homes more frequently. Improvements in the public transport system and the increase in car ownership make it possible for people to travel longer distances to work. Hopes of better housing, more space, opportunities for better jobs have led people to move to new towns and new areas of housing development, leaving the companionship and support of grandparents, aunts, uncles — the extended family — behind. Relatives can be visited from time to time and contact by telephone helps to keep family links open but obviously the range of family contacts is narrowed. In times of family trouble — sickness, unemployment, accident, divorce, old age — the family is more likely to turn to the state for aid than towards relatives.

Families have fallen in size. Parents can now control the size of their family and plan when to have children. Consequently women spend a shorter time in childbearing and have greater freedom to pursue careers and jobs outside the home. Added to this, as technology has advanced in the home there is greater freedom from household drudgery. With wives increasingly assuming the role of joint breadwinner, domestic duties including care and responsibility for children are being shared, in many homes, by both parents.

It has been said that the modern family has moved from being home-centred to being 'child-centred'. Generally parents are more interested in their children now and often have high expectations of them. The family remains the place where the child is treated as a whole person and parents have a deep knowledge of their own children. Both father and mother share responsibilities for child-rearing tasks. It should also be borne in mind that there seems to be an increase in 'child-bashing' — an indication perhaps of the stresses and pressures upon the family today.

Children in any country are brought up within a social framework and have to accept the patterns of behaviour and standards of their parents. In Britain these are based on social conformity to things like cleanliness, politeness ('please', 'thank you', using knives and forks, not grabbing, taking your turn), restraint of aggression, regard for education, respect for property. In other communities the bases of social behaviour may be quite different. Now that Britain is a multi-racial society it is a pity that those of us who work with children do not know more about the cultures of our new citizens because many problems of behaviour in playgroups, nurseries and schools arise through misunderstanding of the things we each separately take for granted.

The strength of any family depends first of all on the relationship between husband and wife, and then on how they see themselves in relation to their immediate community — neighbours, friends, work-mates — and what they find important to work for together. The relationship of his parents to each other is a fundamental factor in the development of each child, though he only becomes aware of this relationship gradually and at first only through the quality of the mothering he gets.

To 'mother' a child has become a useful verb and describes a whole collection of attitudes and actions based on the behaviour of a mother to her child. It should be remembered, however, that some 'mothering' functions may be fulfilled by father.

The little baby does not know his mother as a separate person. He does not see or understand the world clearly; he only knows that he feels contented, warm and safe, or uncomfortable, angry or frightened. His mother is that part of his surroundings which com-forts him, feeds him and makes him feel safe and warm. Loud noises and being dropped or held loosely frighten him and being kept waiting for his food, so that he feels acute discomfort, makes him angry and anxious. His mother knows that he feels these things and she tries to avoid situations which arouse these feelings. The kind of person he will grow up to be depends to a very large extent on how he finds the world in his early baby days. If he feels safe and con-tented more often than he feels abandoned and desperate he will grow up feeling that the world can be trusted and depended on and this will form a secure base for him from which to venture out and experiment in all kinds of ways. This will strengthen his initiative and confidence and he will more readily meet new people and new situa-tions all through his life. His mother tries not to let situations develop which are too much for him. For instance she does not keep him waiting too long for his food and she does not leave him to cry alone until he grows frightened. Of course, though he knows nothing of this, his mother also protects the baby from accident and illness as far as she can by taking sensible precautions such as guarding fires, making sure his pram has good brakes and a cat net, keeping his milk uncontaminated, and in due course taking medical advice about protecting him from dangerous diseases like whooping-cough and diphtheria. She arranges a steady sensible routine of life for him and keeps to it, varying it from time to time to meet new needs as the baby grows, or to meet exceptional circumstances.

When he is a little older his mother plays with the baby when he is awake and talks and sings to him. She shows her joy and delight in him in the way she touches and handles him, in the tones of her voice and in her smile. She prepares him to meet new experiences by her handling of his weaning and later on in his lavatory training. As he grows she provides a safe environment for him to explore and she gives him plenty of simple playthings. She plans his day so that he has time to play with them and she encourages him and plays with him. She talks to him and laughs with him as she goes about her work and later on tells him stories and answers his questions. She gives him as much of her attention as she can while he needs her but as soon as she sees he is ready she makes sure he has children about his own age to play with.

The baby's mother draws his father into companionship with the baby as much as she can, and this relationship becomes more important to the toddler and the young child. The baby's mother is most important to him when he is tiny but if she is sensible she is prepared to remain steadily in the background as he advances into the world and makes new relationships with his father, with other children and with other adults. If the baby's relationship with his mother is firm and sound he will not find it difficult to make these new relationships.

The child feels from early babyhood two sides to his mother's character, one which gives him pleasure (food, warmth, comfort, gentle handling) and one which denies him what he wants (she makes him wait, she refuses him certain things, she puts him to bed when he wants to be nursed or crawl about). When he is a young baby he is not clear that these are two sides of the same person, he is inclined to think that he has a good mother and a harsh mother. He finds it hard as he develops to accept that these two are one because he does not enjoy both loving and hating the same mother. When later on he becomes aware of his father he enjoys being held by his strong hands and carried on his shoulder, but he also realises that this figure backs mother up in her refusals and inhibitions and in a way this makes it easier for him to bear because he now does have two people with whom to separate out his feelings.

We talk a great deal about mothering and the importance of the relationship between a mother and her child and we do not always think about the importance to the child and the family of the father.

The fact that the father is there and is supporting the family is in itself enormously important. It gives the family unit a cohesion, a completeness and an identity. His financial support frees the mother from anxiety and releases her to care for the children in her own way. When we read accounts by social workers of the plight of widows, deserted wives and unmarried mothers struggling to earn a living as well as to make a home for their children we realise some of the burden they bear and the results this has on the family.

More important still is the fact that because he loves her and is hers to love his wife has value in her own eyes. She feels wanted and cherished and this joy she passes on to the children by the way she speaks and moves and touches them. Children are quick to feel happiness or unhappiness between parents and to react to it.

Father is strong and powerful and to a certain extent mysterious because he disappears each day in an important way and is welcomed home again with pleasure, and to the child he gradually assumes more and more authority. At the same time the child much admires his clever father and so discipline is more naturally taken from him. He can turn more easily then to his mother for comfort and cosseting when he needs them. Many fathers these days are away from home a great deal by the nature of their work — they may travel long distances to an office or factory or may be long-distance lorry drivers, salesmen, construction workers, oil-rig workers, others may work awkward or unusual hours — hospital staff, fishermen, dairymen, train and bus drivers, factory shift-workers — so that they do not see much of their children. This means that many decisions and most of the day-to-day discipline falls to the mothers and many mothers are also wage-earners so that children are aware that their father is not the only provider of the family. For all these reasons the father image is not the same as it was in past generations. Nevertheless, whether he is present or not, if the relationship between mother and father is sound then father is a figure of importance and authority, often as much because of his absences as in spite of them. There is a great deal of magic and fantasy involved in a little child's images of his parents because there is so much of life that he knows nothing about and a father who appears from time to time, who is often talked about by mother when he is away and who is obviously important to her, can be a powerful figure, especially if he is a definite sort of person.

Of course his father gives the child a great deal more than authority and discipline. Parents give the child models of behaviour from which the child can learn. Father may give his children a model of strength and skill to copy and a standard to measure other men by. A girl's choice of a husband may be strongly influenced by her admiration or rejection of her father. Parents' social and moral attitudes are extremely important in the formation of children's characters. If a parent is a reliable, honest, kindly person, scrupulous and generous in his relations with neighbours, employers and friends these are the attitudes his children will absorb without question as normal. If, on the other hand, he is untruthful and dishonest even if only in small ways, or selfish and unhelpful, these are the traits his children will take as their pattern. This does not mean to say that the mother's social and moral behaviour is not important. Her behaviour is an earlier and perhaps more fundamental basis for forming the character of her children. If she is an irritable or unstable person, if she cheats the tradespeople and is rude to the neighbours, these things influence the way she speaks and acts and when her children are babies they are conscious of these things and absorb them as part of the world they know and depend on. But when they are two or three years old they are able to observe their parents' behaviour objectively as well as to be influenced unconsciously by it and it is at this stage that their father is becoming important to them.

Their father is also a source of fun and happiness to his children. He takes them out, gives them treats and holidays and teaches them a great many interesting skills: how to dig and make concrete paths and build walls in the garden, how to drive a car, how to throw and catch balls and play games, how to swim and fish and climb.

> Two families whose children were playgroup friends were having tea in the garden and watching four-year-old Caroline and three-year-old Oliver building imaginary houses in the branches of a tree on the lawn. The two fathers were taken aback to see how scrupulously their own methods of carpentry and household repairs had been observed by their children. Caroline put two coats of paint on the wall of her 'house', Oliver put three on his. Caroline nailed her shelves to the wall, Oliver used screws. The gestures and comments of the children, unaware that they were being watched, were quite specific.

As children grow away from their mother and her familiar domestic surroundings their father opens an exciting new world of activity to them. Then they enjoy returning to their mother and the warmth and nourishment of home.

Children need both parents for a good many years. As they grow away from them during the school years they still need their support and encouragement and in adolescence they need understanding and acceptance. During these years from babyhood onwards they become aware that their parents are scaling down as it were. When they are small their parents are so powerful that they are not quite real and every child has a highly distorted view of his own parents; they are much bigger and better than other children's parents and at times much fiercer and more cruel, too. As he grows and meets more and more adults and stands by himself at school and makes his own judgements of the adults he meets, he begins to see his parents as real people in a world of other people and then, perhaps after a period of rejecting them, he is free to make new and more realistic relationships with them.

Pressures on the family

There have always been pressures on families. Strong families have withstood them and become stronger, families not so strong have managed to survive, perhaps not without some casualties, weak families have sometimes broken apart. Some of today's pressures are the same as in other times — anxieties about work and money; housing difficulties; bad health; human temperament — but many are peculiar to this age — loneliness and boredom in new housing estates; separation of young couples from parents and other relatives, the high cost of postage, telephones and travel making contact difficult; constant pressure of advertising to accumulate more and more material goods; the fast pace of life; a continual battering on the senses and mind by the news media of disasters, conflict and violence; overcrowding, congestion, noise and ugliness. Pressures like these often lead to friction, tension and disagreements between husband and wife. Children sense dissension and they become anxious and unhappy. Young children don't understand that arguments are not quarrels and raised voices frighten them. Depressed, dissatisfied, irritable parents find it hard to be warm and loving to their children.

Inexperienced young mothers without the support of older experienced relations are sometimes unable to fulfil the fundamental task of nurturing, guiding and controlling the child successfully. Some support is given by the health visitors but these are not always welcomed into the home and their resources are often grossly over-stretched because of the demands of the area in which they work.

Mothers are often insecure in their dealings with their children; relationships can become tense and fraught with anxiety and this is reflected in the child's attitudes and behaviour. When the child sees little of father there is difficulty in finding a pattern in male behaviour.

If the basic relationship between the parents is not strong, if either partner cannot stand up to the pressures of responsibility, then disaster to the marriage may follow with consequences to the children which may well become the concern of other adults — grandparents, health visitors, social workers, teachers, assistants, playgroup leaders. Some fathers are workshy, some have married so young that the responsibilities of maintaining a home and family become too much for them, they feel trapped, they may break down, become ill, leave home or begin to drink. Some girls are so young and ill-equipped that they cannot cope with babies and home and housekeeping money. They may stop trying and feel defeated and hopeless. In either case the children suffer. The boys have no responsible pattern to follow, the girls never see what a comfort and stimulus a good home can be. The family may get a reputation for shiftlessness which affects the children at school and later on they may find it hard to get jobs.

The child himself may cause pressures within the family. The effect that a child can have on parents is often underestimated. The burden of looking after a handicapped child can cause such severe strain within the family that relationships between husband, wife, brothers and sisters become so warped or damaged that the family structure can break down completely. Disturbed children can cause disturbed parents. Bright, over-active children needing little sleep can have a profound affect on parents causing breakdown in health, anxiety, stress and a disturbance in the relationship between father and mother. Parents have to make a number of adjustments — some of which they may not have foreseen — when a baby is born; they may suffer loss of sleep and privacy, a curtailment of social life and financial hardship.

It is a common belief that poverty does not matter if the family is a loving one but children from poor families can suffer real physical, intellectual and social handicaps. The larger the family the more likely is the possibility of the children living in poverty with parents having the responsibility of more children to feed and clothe. Father may need to supplement his wages by working longer hours and spending less time with his family. Mother, with more domestic responsibilities, will have less time and energy to spend with her children so that they have less encouragement, interest and stimulus from adults in their early years. At school the children will gradually become aware that they are shabbier than their classmates, that their parents are not able to buy expensive school uniforms or PE kit, or pay for their school dinners. They have fewer treats and no holidays to tell about and in extreme cases they may be shunned because they are grubby and smell. Hot water and soap cost money, clothes can't be washed often and there are no others to change into. They can't ask friends home to tea and so they are not asked into other children's homes. There are no birthday parties and few Christmas presents. They may gradually become discouraged or lose confidence and grow aggressive. It takes extraordinary parents to counteract these things and to keep the family together confidently but many manage it magnificently. If teachers and assistants at school understand the pressures of poverty on the children of such families they may be able to help by building up the children's self-respect and sense of their own value in unobtrusive ways.

One-parent families

There is an increasing number of one-parent families in our society. In the majority it is the mother who remains with the children but some fathers are left by death or desertion to manage alone. A mother may be unmarried, deserted, separated or divorced, or her husband may be in prison, incapacitated by accident or illness, or he may have died.

Many one-parent families are happy and successful but it takes a strong and competent parent to manage it. There are worries about money and accommodation. Some women marry without having been trained for work that pays well and so they can earn little. Landlords dislike letting to single parents. It is exhausting to do a full-time job and give time and care to the children as well as keeping up with the household chores. All decisions have to be taken alone; all the discipline as well as all the love has to come from the one parent who often feels depressed, resentful and lonely. It is hard to make the extra effort needed to take part in parent–teacher or play-group activities, yet these things are valuable for the children's welfare. There is little time to have a day out or time to oneself and there is a temptation to depend too much on the children for comfort.

It is not surprising that children from families such as these are often tense and difficult and find it hard to concentrate at school. It is admirable that so many are secure, healthy and happy.

In families where parents divorce or separate the children have to bear the grief of parting from a parent they may love dearly before they can understand what has happened. They may feel it is somehow their fault. If a parent dies not only are the children shocked and bewildered but they may find that the other parent withdraws from them in grief for a while and this is a double blow, very frightening to little children. These are all things we should be aware of when the families of children we work with face a crisis.

Day nurseries and, where they exist, day-care centres are designed to help one-parent families by leaving them free to work during the day. Day-care centres are rare in Britain but fulfil a useful function in some other countries. They care for children under school age all day, providing for them a nursery-school type of programme, and look after school children before school, during the lunch break and after school. Meals are provided and games and workshop activities are organised. Some day-care centres I have seen in America and Canada involve voluntary help from the community to supplement the work of the professional staff; others prefer not to do this.

A great many single parents depend on childminders for help, either for all-day care of under-fives or for after-school care of older children. Childminders sometimes cooperate with playgroups or nursery schools (see p. 146).

Adults with children in care

A child may come into the care of a local authority at the request of parents who are not able to care for him themselves, or on the authority of a court. When very young children come into care the social services departments try to place them in foster homes rather than in Community Homes or residential nurseries. There are now few residential nurseries in the country, though some of the voluntary societies and some county councils still maintain them. Community Homes are usually small with a group of children of different ages living as a family with resident social workers. Often there is a married couple as Head, sometimes with the husband doing his own work outside the Home, and assistant house parents either living in or coming daily.

Although most babies and young children are boarded out some do come into Homes either because there are no suitable foster homes available or because brothers and sisters from the same family are taken into care at the same time and it is best to keep them together.

House parents

The staff in Homes for children in care have a variety of roles to play and some of them are complicated. This is not the place to discuss them in any detail because the subject is too big, we can only try to see some of the factors involved. It is convenient to use the pronoun 'she' in the discussion but of course the considerations apply equally to male resident social workers.

The Head of a Community Home spends a great deal of her time in planning for the welfare of the children. She is the liaison officer for them with the local authority (or with the voluntary body and the Department of Health and Social Security). She is the admini-strator within the Home. She arranges for the day-to-day main-tenance of the building and its cleaning. She plans decorations, furniture and fittings; she plans meals and orders supplies. She interviews and helps to train staff, she arranges with them their duties, off-times and holidays. She knows that a contented staff with a sense of purpose is more likely to make a happy atmosphere for the children. She sets the standards of policy and routines. She is responsible for the safety and health of the children and for their happiness.

But the very young child in the Home knows and understands little of all the care for him that concerns the Head. For him it is the moment-to-moment care which is his life: the touch of a hand, the tone of a voice, a cuddle and a game in the bath, the answer to a question, a leisurely tucking-up in bed, in short, the immediate rela-tionship that exists between him and his house mother. Whether the touch of her hand is gentle and the tone of her voice loving may depend to a great extent on the wise leadership of the Head, but the child does not recognise this and depends for his security on the facts of his house mother's care for him.

It would seem at first as if the role that the house mother with little children has to play is straightforward. We would think that she only has to reproduce the attitudes and responses of the real mother as closely as she can. But her role is more complicated than this. Some of the children in her group will have come into care as new babies and will have known no other mothering. To these she will be the mother they have never known. Others of the children will come into care at two, three or four years of age on the break-up of their family and have conscious and subconscious memories of their own mothers and their personalities will be deeply influenced by the mothering they have had from them. Towards these children the house mother will be able to behave in a motherly way but if she is wise she will not expect the same response from them as she has from the babies. These newcomers may be suspicious or hostile towards her because she supplants their own mothers, or they feel that she does. She may have barriers to their trust to overcome or to accept and if their mothers treated them in ways different from her ways or expected different behaviour from them from the behaviour she expects from them this may lead to stubbornness or obstinacy or resentful behaviour. If they have a parent or relatives who can keep in touch with them the house mother must try to keep the memory of them fresh and alive by talking about them between their visits. Their house mother is the immediate link between the children and their friends outside the Home and the way she talks to them when they visit the children and their response to her is important to each child. They must approve of each other so that the child feels safe. This is much harder in practice than in theory.

Despite the complications, the role of the resident worker is closer to that of a natural mother than that of nursery nurses or assistants in other types of work, so her understanding of mothering must be strong enough to help her overcome as many of the problems of institutional life as she can. She is dealing with children in an unnatural situation. For instance, she must share the responsibility of her group of children with several helpers since, unlike an ordinary mother, she is not on duty for twenty-four hours a day; in a residential nursery she often has no father-figure to take the masculine share of authority and to give masculine leadership and encouragement to the children; the children are frequently anxious and unhappy and have special behaviour problems; in some cases they have been introduced to too many other children at too early an age and she knows that unless she can build up with each child in her group a sound personal relationship he may begin to treat other children as objects of no consequence to be used for his purposes instead of as people to love and care for. This relationship with her will be the bridge he must cross to a full share in the life of the community. If he cannot communicate with her he may not be able to communicate with the world beyond her.

There may also be in her group some of the young children who are in care for only a short time to bridge a period of crisis in their homes. Here her role is a different one again. The house mother in this case is a temporary mother figure and she must keep the child's own mother and family firmly present in his mind. She may have the child's shock and anxiety at sudden separation to cope with and she may, as the days go by, have also to prepare him for a new baby or the loss of one of the family when he goes back home.

Older children in a Home can begin to understand that good administration is a form of care but even so it is still the personal relationship with house parents which is of the greatest importance. They need their house parents to take an interest in their school life, to take pleasure in their clothes and their appearance, to help them to entertain their friends, to give them thoughtfully selected presents for birthdays and Christmas, to have a fund of ideas for games and fun, to share TV programmes and records, to be ready to listen to them, to respect their private possessions and to leave them alone when they want to be undisturbed.

Because they are older and have some command of language, it may be easier for these children to talk about their anxieties and resentments than it is for the younger children who still cannot talk well, but in practice it is seldom easy. They often have a poor vocabulary and are not adept at expressing their feelings in words; language is not a flexible tool for them. So they may show they are disturbed, resentful and anxious by swearing, eating messily, stealing, being noisy and destructive or obstinate and obstructive. Part of the house parent's business is to understand and accept that this behaviour is an expression of an inarticulate child's confusion and unhappiness. Even if he can talk well a child may not want to discuss his feelings with adults he does not know well or whom he distrusts or resents. It may take a long time before a child can build up a relationship of trust with a house parent so that he can talk about his grief and worry. When he can, and when he finds that words help him to sort out the things that beset him, he finds that he can cope with them gradually on a realistic basis and this frees him to develop in other ways: at school, with the other children in the Home and with relatives outside. The fact that relationships of this kind are slow to mature makes it all the more important that there should not be frequent changes of staff in Homes.

Another important part of the work of house parents is to provide for the children's play and leisure activities. This does not mean only swimming and football but material and opportunities to make things, to work with carpentry and paints and clay, to dress up, to cook, to sew and knit, to experiment with sand and water, to make music. The healing value of achieving something by one's own efforts, of creating something out of mess, of overcoming the innate problems of materials and tools, is without price to hurt and unhappy children. It is an essential of life. To give the children this kind of play means setting aside room for it, keeping a careful balance between chaos and control, being ready to teach a skill and then letting the child work by himself, giving time and encouragement and being prepared for failure and disappointment.

Not all house parents are aware of the value of play and their own concern for the children sometimes leads them into denying them the joy of achievement. On a visit to a Home I watched a slightly backward three-year-old boy trying with great concentration to manoeuvre his wooden truck through the open french window. The wheels would stick on the metal sill. He carefully backed it off and tried tipping it sideways. A kindly house mother, passing by, gave him a cheery word and lifted the truck outside for him. He brought it back inside, getting it successfully over the sill, and tried again to get it out. Another house parent came up, patted him lovingly and lifted the truck outside. He patiently brought it in and tried again to work out the problem of the inside sill. But when the first house mother came back and said briskly 'Stuck again, love?' and put the truck outside he gave up. I hoped he would have a tantrum but he sat drearily doing nothing.

Of course everybody in and about a Home for children is impor-tant — the cook, her kitchen helpers, the cleaners, gardeners, secretaries. Each has a contribution and a skill to offer to the children and each presents an opportunity for a new relationship to form and for further communication between the children and the community to grow.

Foster parents

Foster parents are ordinary people who want to share their homes with disadvantaged children on either a short-term or a long-term basis. The social services departments of local authorities place children in homes they think are suitable for them and pay a modest board for each child. There are a number of reasons why people want to take foster children. It is not an easy job. It goes on for twenty-four hours a day, seven days a week, cuts out much social life and demands great stores of patience, tolerance and affection, so reasons for undertaking it must be strong. Perhaps either the husband or wife was rejected or unhappy as a child and wants to help other children in the same position. Or the couple may be childless and feel their marriage is incomplete without children. They may want companions for an only child of their own or their own children are growing up and they feel they could use the skills they learned as parents in giving time and affection to foster children. Or it may be that they have read of the need for foster homes and think they could help by taking a child to share family life with their own growing children.

It is essential that husband and wife should agree about taking the step of fostering children and both be prepared to share the added work load and stress it brings. Most couples think carefully before undertaking it and try to weigh up what it will entail. They wisely discuss it with their older children and explain to the younger ones what is going to happen.

Foster parents are willing to take on for the children in their care the roles of real parents as far as this is possible but it is inevitable that they should be unprepared for some of the emotional crises that arise when the foster children are placed with them. They may be baffled by a complete lack of response in the foster child, though they may have been warned by the social worker that this is likely to happen. Sometimes a foster child is very quiet and amenable for some weeks and then, when he begins to feel secure in his new home, he lets himself go and expresses his feelings of resentment and hate at the way life has treated him by behaving in a thoroughly difficult and disagreeable way. This phase may last a long time and foster parents may find their willingness to understand and accept him strained almost unbearably so that they begin to feel they have failed the child and have made a mistake in undertaking the task of fostering. If they can manage to continue to accept the bad behaviour and still give the child affection they will have done him a great service and the trying behaviour may clear up as he feels he can get along without it. Experienced foster parents know that this can happen but it can shatter confidence in those undertaking the work for the first time and they need much help and support from the social worker concerned with the placement.

The reactions of their own children sometimes surprise and even shock foster parents. Their children may clearly dislike the foster child, or, after some time of accepting him, they may suddenly become acutely jealous and demand more attention. This puts an extra strain on the parents who must try to be fair and loving to each child. Sometimes their children are embarrassed by the way the foster child behaves at school or in the street or shops, or when friends are present and they may show their disapproval by contempt or unkindness. On the other hand friendship may grow between the foster child and a child of the family and it sometimes happens that a very young child taken into a family with much older children will cling to a daughter rather than to the mother and for some time will only be comforted and cared for by her.

Another thing that foster parents at first do not take into consideration, and which may disconcert them, is the strength of the child's wish to be back with his own family no matter how cruelly they may have rejected or ill-treated him. Often the child's mind refuses to remember the true facts of his former life and he day-dreams about kind and loving parents. Even if he does not do this, his strong desire is to be in his own home even if it no longer exists and this can be a difficult thing for foster parents to accept, it seems so unreasonable. But reason enters very little into the intense feelings of rejected children.

It is important that all the adults concerned in the child's care should realise how necessary it is to him that he should be helped to keep in touch with all the people who have mattered to him throughout his life. This means that the foster parents must try all the time to talk to him about his relations or any other foster parents he may have had and, if he returns eventually to his home, that his parents should be encouraged to talk in a friendly way about the foster parents. It would be a good thing if he could visit his former foster parents from time to time with his parents' approval.

Another hazard which may arise concerns visits by the child's real mother or other relatives. The foster mother may, to her own dismay, find that she dislikes the natural mother and finds it hard to look forward with pleasure to her visits. If the child's mother con-stantly breaks promises to visit, or forgets a birthday, or tells the child lies, the foster mother may find herself growing indignant and angry when she sees the hurt and disappointment of the child. On the other hand the natural mother may become jealous of the foster mother, and, because she feels inadequate and guilty, she may behave in a hostile or unpleasant manner. This situation can put the child in an intolerable position and the foster parents in a dilemma. They must respect the child's feeling for his own mother and they know that to compete with his mother in any way for his loyalty must be wrong. Somehow they have to see him over the bad time without betraying their own anger. The social workers making the placement in the first place will have taken a disturbed mother into account and have chosen the foster family with great care so that the foster parents know they can rely on support in their difficulty.

If the foster child proves unresponsive for a long time despite all her efforts to make him feel wanted, or if his behaviour continues to be difficult, the foster mother may become depressed and anxious and wonder whether she should ask for the child to be taken away. Her husband may dislike seeing her overworked and worried and may want to give up the project. At this point the social worker may be able to help by reassuring them that they are doing better than they realise and she may be able to arrange for a discussion with a group of other foster parents. Like all parents they can be reassured by finding that many problems are common to all families and the behaviour that so much concerns them is not caused by their poor handling of the situation but by the circumstances which first brought the child into care. If for any reason the fostering of a child has to end it is important that everyone should appreciate what has been good in the fostering. This is never lost.

Many children are happy and settled within their foster family with whom they make lifelong ties. Severe problems do not arise, but it is the unexpected emotional reaction which can be unsettling even to experienced foster parents. One mother who was most successfully bringing up a foster daughter whom she had taken into her own family as a baby said, 'Lately I am shocked and ashamed to find I hate the social worker who comes to visit us. We have been good friends for years and she has helped a lot but now quite suddenly I don't want her to come into my house.' She may have felt that the social worker's visits were a reminder that the little girl was not really her own but whatever the reason was she was a sensible woman and realised that if she relaxed and did not try to fight her revulsion the mood would pass.

Foster parents perform a service of very great value to the community. They differ in their skills. Some are best with children who only need short periods of foster care to help them over a crisis in their own family. Others are skilful with disturbed children, others enjoy caring for handicapped children, others again like best to take young teenagers. When a child will need a long period of fostering, probably for all his childhood, it is best for him to be placed as a baby but this is not always possible and many foster parents have given love and a full happy family life to children who first came to them as toddlers or during their first years of school.

Further reading

Bell, Lorna, *Underprivileged Underfives*, Ward Lock Educ., 1976.
Bowley, Agatha H., *Child Care*, Livingstone, 1951.
Burlingham, D. and Freud, A., *Infants Without Families*, 2nd edn, Allen & Unwin, 1965, particularly Chapter 5.
Flint, Betty M., *The Child and the Institution*, University of London Press, 1967.
Parfit, Jessie, ed., *The Community's Children*, Longman, 1967.

Rutler, M., *Maternal Deprivation Re-assessed*, Penguin, 1972.

Social Services Departments of Local Authorities, pamphlets and circulars on fostering.

Tod, Robert, ed., *Social Work in Foster Care*, Longman, 1971.

Wedge, P. and Prosser, H., *Born to Fail*, Arrow Books, 1973.

Winnicott, D. W., *The Child, the Family and the Outside World*, Penguin: Pelican, 1964, particularly Part One, and Part Two, 17 and 28.

Woodhead, M., *Intervening in Disadvantage: a challenge for nursery education*, N.F.E.R., 1976.

Young, M. and Wilmott, P., *The Symmetrical Family*, Routledge and Kegan Paul, 1973.

See also Barnardo's Social Work Papers, Barnardo Publications Ltd, Ilford, Essex IG6 1QG.

Chapter 8

The role of the adult II

Child-minders

The daily minding of other people's children is neither new nor peculiar to this generation. Neighbours have always helped each other in this natural and sensible way and in some of the extended family groups of other countries the children hardly know who are their mothers and who are their aunts. But since the beginning of the machine age the practice has grown in industrial cities where women work outside their homes. In nineteenth-century England older women minded the children while their mothers worked in the mills. Today it is variously estimated that between 150,000 and 200,000 children are looked after in this country by professional child-minders.

We now know enough about the needs of children to be concerned about the quality of daily minding; Parliament passed the Nurseries and Child-minders Regulation Act in 1948 and amended it in 1968 and 1970 so that there should be some standards of care. The social services departments of local authorities administer the Act and certificates of registration are issued when the department is satisfied about elementary standards of safety in the home, about the health of the daily minder and her household, and about her suitability to undertake the care of other people's babies and young children.

A person who, in her own home, looks after someone else's pre-school child for more than two hours a day for payment or reward is required to be registered but parents make their own arrangements with the child-minder and the fee is negotiated between them and is not the concern of the authority. Close relatives, like grandparents, aunts or older sisters are not required to register, and no registration is needed by women who only care for children of school age. Nannies, au pair girls or baby-sitters are not child-minders in the legal sense because they work in the employer's house and not in their own, though if nannies and others employed in looking after children also look after other people's pre-school children and these people make payments for this service, then the nanny or baby-sitter should be registered.

Mothers in full-time employment and fathers caring for families on their own need to arrange for their babies and young children to be cared for all day and their young school children to be looked after in the afternoons and in the holidays. The parents who choose child-minders rather than day nurseries do so for various reasons. One is, of course, that there are not enough day nurseries or day-care centres; another is that many parents genuinely believe that a home atmosphere is better than an institution for their little children. They are looking for a kind, welcoming mother substitute. Sometimes, unfortunately, they are not prepared for the jealousy they feel if their child becomes very fond of the child-minder. This sometimes leads to a child being changed from one child-minder to another several times.

Child-minders are performing a useful service and they are often hard-working and careful. As in all areas of work, some are slovenly and incompetent or ignorant and these are often those who have evaded registration because their houses are not suitable, or they take too many children, or they do not want to submit to visits from the local authority's officers. The local authorities find these illegal minders difficult to locate because they usually live in overcrowded areas of large cities.

A great deal of criticism has been levelled at child-minding and this is usually based on reports of what goes on among the unregistered minders when it is discovered but even so, among registered minders there are some who do not understand the needs of young children beyond giving them food and shelter so that the children they mind are bored and deprived of mental stimulus and the opportunities they need for play. Registration in itself does not make a good child-minder and there are no doubt good unregistered child-minders.

The Act requires, in effect, that the child-minder's house shall be safe, warm and clean and that the outside play space shall be safely fenced but each local authority may interpret the Act as they see fit and make their own local regulations. Local authorities differ about the number of children a child-minder may take and it depends to some extent on the accommodation she has; a number of authorities say not more than three children under five years including her own if the minder works by herself and not more than seven if she has a helper. If she provides food for the children it must be suitable for them and she must have an adequate kitchen in which to prepare it. Part of the duty of the local authority is to visit the homes of registered child-minders, partly to see that these standards are maintained but also to give help and encouragement.

As a community we were slow to recognise the service child-minders were providing and to give them enough positive help. As with all mothers of young children it can be a lonely job which by its very nature cuts the women off from contact with each other and from community groups. Much more is now being done to help. Playmaterial libraries have been set up in a number of areas and playgroups have helped by encouraging local child-minders to bring the children to the playgroup and involving them in watching and helping. When they see how children play and realise how simply they could give them similar opportunities at home they are enthusiastic and happy to learn more. Local authorities have subsidised playgroup visitors who take material, books, toys and suggestions for play into the homes of child-minders, play for a little while with the children, tell them stories, show them books and pictures and sing with them. In some areas these visitors invite the child-minders to coffee mornings organised like the excellent Mother and Toddler Clubs where the mothers chat and exchange ideas or listen to a talk over their coffee while the children play under supervision at the other end of the room. In one area the Preschool Playgroups Association offers several places for child-minders on its courses for playgroup helpers. These courses are concerned with simple practical ideas for play, the exchange of ideas and, inevitably, the discussion of things that worry or puzzle members of the group as well as the things they have discovered about children and the things they have enjoyed doing with them. The National Association of Child-minders collects and disperses information and encourages the setting up of more toy and book libraries. Belonging to such an organisation helps a child-minder to feel part of a body of people doing a useful community service.

One reason why child care of this kind is often so deficient in stimulus for the children is that the parents themselves are unaware of the value of rich play for children and therefore they do not enquire about it when they place the children with the minder. If they saw their children happily occupied in the home of the minder they might be more likely to provide suitable play material for them at home and so the value of help given to the minders would spread further.

It goes without saying that there should always be close coopera-tion between parents and those who mind their children. One hopes that the child is taken several times to visit the minder before being left with her all day so that he knows that mother approves of the person in the house and is friendly with her. Likes and dislikes about food, sleeping habits and the use of the lavatory should be discussed and agreed on, a favourite toy or blanket could be taken along each day and action to be taken in the event of accident or illness decided. If both adults, the parent and the child-minder, try to see each other's point of view and talk over their problems friction, which can only be harmful to the child may be avoided. Parents should also talk about the events of the day with the child and encourage him to tell what he has done so that he knows his parents think about him while they are apart and that he is not abandoned.

In the day nursery and family centre

Day nurseries in this country are usually maintained by the department of social services of the local authority (city or county council) and children between the ages of one month and five years are admitted on social or medical grounds to be looked after for the greater part of each working day by a trained staff. The reasons for admission to day nurseries are usually poor housing, the necessity for the mother to work, the disability of one or both parents or the necessity to provide some relief for an overburdened single parent in a situation where this may save the family from breaking up.

The work of the matron in a day nursery is similar in some respects to that of the Head of a residential Home but different in some others. She is responsible for the day-to-day maintenance of the building and its cleanliness, for the care of furniture, fittings and materials, for the planning of meals and the ordering of supplies. She is also responsible for the routine of the nursery, the setting of standards and the arrangement of staff duties. Here, however, is one difference between the work of a day nursery and that of a residential nursery or a Community Home. The staff of a day nursery does not work at night or at weekends and so their hours of duty are constant, the children have fewer daily changes of staff and the matron has a less complicated timetable of duties to prepare.

On the other hand one of the matron's greatest responsibilities is to work closely with the parents of the children. All the children who attend a day nursery go home in the afternoons, their true centre is their home. If the two halves of their lives are not harmonious, if their mothers and the nursery staff do not respect each other, the children suffer. They are bewildered by cross-currents of feeling between the adults who control the two halves of their life. Some parents feel guilty about not being able to provide an adequate home for their children even though it may be through no fault of theirs, and this makes them defensive in their attitude towards the nursery staff. They sometimes suspect that the staff are critical of them and, indeed, sometimes this is true, so that feelings of hostility and resentment are clear for the children to sense, and children, however young, are quick to perceive feelings of this kind. Their trust in the nursery staff may be undermined and they feel unsafe and unhappy.

Some of the mothers of children in day nurseries are young unmarried girls who have had no time to learn to be practical and no experience of responsibility. They are themselves often shocked and hurt and find the details of earning a living for themselves and their children difficult and exhausting. They need imaginative and friendly support from the nursery staff and a true respect for the effort they are making. Almost every mother (or father) with a child in a day nursery has a number of severe problems to struggle with and the fact that she has entered her child in the nursery and is making the effort, sometimes a considerable effort, to bring him each day means that she wants the best conditions for him and is aware that the nursery can supply them. This is a good basis for respect and confidence on both sides. It is hardly necessary to say that practical matters like the introduction of mixed feeding and lavatory training are always carried out by close cooperation between mother and nursery staff.

A danger in day nursery care about which the matron is aware and tries to make her staff aware is the temptation to be content to 'mind' the children. This is a subtle danger and arises from the very fact that the children are there only during working hours and the real responsibility for them lies with their parents. It is easy for members of staff to feel that all they need to do is to keep the children safe and clean, to feed them, and to let them sleep. It is part of the responsibility of the matron to encourage her staff and students to observe the children, to understand them and to provide an active stimulus for them in play, in conversation and in care. These very young children meet too many strangers too soon and have to learn to become one of a group too early in their lives. This may do them a great deal of harm so individual relationships are important for each child. The grief and anxiety of a toddler left by his mother among strangers is not a problem in a book about how to care for children, it is an immediate vital fact there among them and some member of staff must respond to it with warmth and gentleness. The child can learn this way that the world outside his home can be comforting and helpful and not cold and cruel.

In a day nursery there can be a steady daily contact between particular members of staff and a group of children so that they get to know each other. A nursery nurse can try to behave towards a young baby much as his mother does. In practical terms this means she lifts the baby steadily and holds him firmly and gently while she dresses and undresses him, bathes him and changes his napkins. She knows that slow confident handling reassures him. She holds him closely and comfortably and gives him her whole attention while she gives him his bottle and she talks and sings to him a good deal while she sees to his needs during the day. It takes planning and discipline to look after each baby in this way when there are a number to be cared for and the relaxed nurse can do it more easily than the tense or irritated one. So staff relationships and the atmosphere of the nursery are both important because of their influence on individual staff members.

Another way in which the nursery nurse in the day nursery undertakes the responsibility of the little child's mother is in stimulating and encouraging him to talk. The second year of a child's life is a critical time for him in this respect and if the staff of the nursery are too busy or too unobservant to talk and sing to him and to take time to listen and respond to his efforts to talk to them the child may not afterwards be able to communicate fully in speech, and he may find it more than usually difficult to read later on in school. Language may never become a useful tool for him.

Play for the older babies and the two- to five-year-old children is so important that only nursery assistants thoroughly trained in how to meet the needs of children at each stage of development should be employed in day nurseries. The bad days of clean floors and few toys have gone but often funds for buying play material for day nurseries are still scanty compared with the funds available for nursery schools. Unless the staff are convinced of the importance of play material of the right kind at each stage this problem is not easily solved.

Recently some local authorities have been replacing or supplementing the day nurseries by family centres — sometimes called 'drop-in centres'. Several of the voluntary bodies (for instance, the National Children's Homes and the Church of England Children's Society) have set up similar centres.

Because of increasing unemployment and the extra pressures it brings, many families and single parents find difficulties in making a secure and loving home for their children. Setting up family centres is an attempt to help such families by providing a friendly place where parents and children can find companionship and help.

A mother, father or both parents may bring their children two or three times a week for a whole day. Meals are provided, the parents paying for their own, the children's usually free.

Teaching of skills (such as making and mending playthings , playing with children, cooking, dressmaking, home repairs) is provided and parents are encouraged to take advantage of this, and to take part in discussions.

The parents are introduced to local toddlers' clubs and playgroups so that in time they will no longer need the support of the family centre. Information is given to them about such organisations as Gingerbread Groups and Parents Anonymous, this last especially for those parents who fear they may be driven to harm their children.

The staff responsible for the day-to-day running of family centres are trained in child care and social work but voluntary workers with special skills to share also take part.

In the nursery school

It is often said that nursery schools should be 'as homelike as possible'. In the sense that they should be safe, warm, loving places that is true, but it is also true that a great deal of the value of a nursery school is that it is *not* the child's home. We cannot remain safe at home all our lives and the healthy young child is ready to make his first step into life outside his home by about three years of age.

In playgroups and nursery schools he meets grown-ups who provide him with new and exciting experiences. In some ways these adults are like his mother. They are kind to him and comfort him when he is hurt or frightened and they give him food and other good things. But they are loving in a different way from his mother's way. They have a lot of children to look after, they are much more objective in their attitude to him and this sets him free in a way he can never be free from his mother. In these groups the intense feelings he has towards his mother can be put aside for a while and he can explore all the new and interesting play material and observe and investigate all the new and interesting behaviour of the other children. He can copy them and so try out a wide variety of behaviour.

A nursery school is a place designed for young children and much thought and planning has gone into the building and equipping of it. The Head is a trained teacher and has a thorough knowledge of the development of children. She knows how to observe them and see what each child needs at his stage of maturity.

In much the same way as the matron of the day nursery she has a good deal of administrative work to do and she is responsible for planning the work and responsibilities of her staff. Ultimately the responsibility for the welfare and safety of the children is hers but if she is wise she sees this as an opportunity for leadership. Each member of her staff has a special contribution to make to the nursery school community according to her gifts and interests and the head teacher can encourage and inspire them all so that each brings her abilities to the work of the whole. She may have students or young assistants to train and her leadership must be such as brings out the best in these adolescent workers. They have a genuine desire to work with children and a generous warmth towards them. The sensible head recognises this and works together with the older staff to guide these attitudes into disciplined channels. They teach the young workers, by example and by discussion, how to watch the children and how to use their imagination towards them so that they can see, even if only to a limited extent, how the nursery and its life appear to the children. This insight into the world of the child does not come easily to most people and even to those willing to make the attempt it takes constant discipline and effort. This is not only true of young students; mature but inexperienced assistants in training find the same difficulties. Our own feelings and prejudices and experiences tend to get in the way of our perception and distort or misinterpret what we see and hear. It is easier to make generalisations ('all three-year-olds do such-and-such') and fit all the children to them than to watch each child and accept him as a person with his own gifts and needs.

It would be easy to list the practical things that nursery assistants do to make the nursery school safe and stimulating for the children — the regular inspection of apparatus and play material, the constant check on renewals and repairs and the addition of new material, vigilance about cleanliness without fussiness, the steady functioning of orderly routine — but this is the normal background of a good nursery school which it is not difficult for assistants to understand and put into practice. More difficult to learn is what not to do. The good nursery school assistant is skilful at being quiet in a positive way. A wise head teacher once said that this was doing nothing, creatively. She meant that the staff in a nursery school should be with the children as a background to their activities, alert to what is going on all around them, not always busy with the children but ready to move into the foreground briefly to anticipate a need, to make a suggestion, to prevent an accident.

There are times when a member of staff must be actively busy, setting out material, washing milk mugs, sorting laundry, telling a story, singing with a group, helping the children with some project, gardening, tidying shelves or mending toys but there are other times when she stands and watches, not idly but relaxed and yet with all her senses alert. She is aware of what the children are doing because she knows them well and can anticipate changes in mood and interest. By a quiet word she can often deflect a child's attention from what may become an explosive situation or she can recognise the exact moment when it is right to introduce a new idea or give a fresh addition to play material. She does not interfere with the children's play but she is ready to discuss it with them when they want her to and she can often be ahead of them in their planning so that she is ready with the next suggestion for an extension of their play when they come to her for help. If she has the imagination to grasp the problems they meet in their play as they see them then she is ready to present to them the raw material for a solution at the right moment. It is not her function to give the solution but only to restate the problem, often in practical terms of additional material or a brief discussion of method. Fortunately in these days most nursery schools have rich resources of music, books and material for the staff to draw on.

Most nursery assistants do not need reminding that the nursery years are important ones in the child's grasp of communication. Young children communicate with others in a good many ways — in their choice of play, in their make-believe, in their painting and building, in their attitudes to adults and other children and, of course, in language. It is in language that they need stimulus and encouragement in these early years because this is the method of communication they will need in later life. The staff of the nursery school have an almost unrivalled opportunity for this stimulus without strain or artificiality. Children who are happy and busy like to talk and are eager to discuss their play. They only do this, however, with adults who treat them seriously, and respect their play. It is easier to talk *at* children than to listen to them and talk *with* them and sometimes nursery assistants have to be reminded about this. Telling stories, reading aloud, sharing songs and finger-plays are all ways in which we have fun but they are also good ways to encourage the use of language. Children need to build not only a large vocabulary but a flexible one. Asking and answering questions is another way we help with this. When children ask us questions we have to listen carefully and try to answer what they ask. This may sound an obvious thing to say but it is not quite as obvious as it seems. In the first place grown-ups often don't really listen to what children ask, partly because they don't wait to ask until we are composed and quiet: they ask when they need to know and this may be when we are busy with something else. Then they can't always express what it is they want to know; they either haven't the words or they are not clear about concepts and are confused about the problem they want solved. We often have to clear the issue before we discover what the real question is. A three-year-old English child in an Australian nursery school, looking at a picture of a paddock in which there were some cows and some watermelons growing asked, 'Why don't the cows sit on these?' (indicating the watermelons). The nursery teacher was so taken aback by this question that she could only think of saying, 'Why do you think they should sit on the watermelons?' This was the best thing she could have said because the child replied 'To keep the calves warm' and this gave the teacher the clue to the child's reasoning. He was used to seeing his mother's hens sitting on clutches of eggs to hatch them and he thought watermelons on the ground were cows' eggs. When we are reasonably sure that we know what it is the child is asking we can give him an honest answer, not so detailed that it will bewilder or bore him but with enough fact to satisfy his immediate need. When he wants more information he will come back. If we don't know the answer we say so but we can suggest ways of finding out: asking someone who may know, looking it up in a book, or trying to find out by experimenting.

Adults working with young children often forget to explain situations to them. They do this partly because they are not using their imagination. Without overstressing the matter or being emotional it is a good idea to discuss with a child something which seems to be puzzling or troubling him. Mark was a quiet, timid little boy who took a long time to take part in the activities of the nursery school. He used to sit in a corner watching the other children, saying little and usually holding one of his own toys in his hand or on his lap. After some time he made friends with another boy, Sam, and for some months they played together contentedly. Then Sam's father was posted to another area and his family moved suddenly. The two families did not know each other and no one thought to explain to Mark what had happened. At first he seemed only to be lonely but then his paintings, which had shown delightful gaiety and colour, became scrappy and dark and he again talked very little. After a long time he began to talk to a new child in the nursery, a little girl called Joan, and they became friends and played together. Joan developed into a happy, composed member of the nursery community and drew Mark into a good deal of group play, although he rarely joined a group unless Joan was there as well. He painted freely and with great maturity, he loved listening to stories and even took a cheerful part in musical activities. Then Joan caught a bad cold and her mother kept her away from the nursery for several days. On the second day of her absence the head teacher noticed Mark sitting in a corner with his outdoor coat on. He had obviously gone to the cloakroom and put it on. When she suggested that he would be more comfortable without it he just shook his head. He refused to eat any dinner or even to come to the table. He looked so ill that the teacher took him on to her lap and began to talk quietly to him while she decided whether to take his temperature and to telephone his mother. She said: 'I'm sorry you aren't feeling well. We miss our children when they have to stay in bed. Joan's mummy says her cold is getting better and she can come back to the nursery tomorrow or the next day. So I hope you won't be sick when she comes back.' She did not think he was listening to her and she was surprised when after a few minutes he got down from her lap, took his coat off and went to the easel and began to paint. He never talked about the incident but the teacher, puzzling over it, began to understand what had happened and how, after the unexplained loss of one companion, Mark was overcome with fear at the disappearance of another. Life was proved to be insecure and terrifying when loved friends could just cease to exist. She realised that only a few words of explanation could have saved so much suffering and although he was an unusually sensitive child this must also be true with all children.

Although explanations help a great deal in many situations there are differences between the way adults and children think and the way they see things that only maturity can reconcile. For instance, one difference between young children and adults is in their grasp of time. Adults can see the whole day in their mind and see it as a pattern of things to be done. Young children live from minute to minute and can only plan ahead for short periods. This can lead to conflict because adults know that some things, like putting play material away, have to begin at a certain time so that other things, like setting dinner-tables or putting out beds, can be done. Children can't see why the play material has to be put away and this situation has to be handled with understanding and tact. On the other hand children gladly accept a regular routine for each day as part of the bounds that set them free. As the child grows older this problem grows less and the child in the primary school becomes aware of timetable demands, though he often needs reminding about getting ready in time for the next activity.

There are other people always about in a nursery school, the cook, the cleaners, gardeners from the parks department, the nurse, advisory teachers, the N.N.E.B. course tutor and, of course, other children's mothers. Most of these people become familiar, so children in a nursery school are aware of many adult roles. The cook can be an important person who welcomes children from time to time into her warm and fragrant kitchen, discusses the equipment with them and helps them to bake their dough shapes. The gardeners use interesting tools and work and talk in a masculine way.

But nursery schools also tend to have a great many less familiar visitors — medical students, playgroup leaders and helpers, health visitors and social workers in training, college lecturers, research workers, comprehensive school pupils, overseas teachers. Nursery school teachers know that the experience of seeing a good nursery school in action is necessary and valuable to all these people but they also know that unless the visitors behave sensibly they can disrupt the children's play. Perhaps there could be some form of briefing for all visitors to nursery schools, setting out the reasons for requiring unobtrusive behaviour, suggesting ways of observing and ways of responding to advances by the children.

Another responsibility for the staff of nursery schools is the decision to accept a proportion of handicapped children. This is a knotty problem because the value of becoming part of a nursery school community is so great for the handicapped child and his parents that teachers are loth to refuse them and doctors, health visitors and social workers are anxious for them to be accepted. But it is clear that the ratio of handicapped to ordinary children must be low: it is usually agreed that there should not be more than one handicapped child to ten normal children and even this ratio must be lower if the handicap of any child is so serious that more adult time and care than usual needs to be given to him.

Nursery school children usually accept and absorb handicapped children into the group without fuss. But what is most important is that doctors should give careful and specific help to the teachers and assistants caring for the group into which the handicapped child will enter by explaining what the limits of the child's abilities are and how these affect his mental model of the world and consequently much of his behaviour. For instance a partially sighted child may be able to see two separate bits of the teacher's face but have no idea that they are parts of the same whole. If the teacher and her assistants understand these limits they can more easily prevent frustrations and misunderstandings for him. They can place material where he can manipulate it, stand or sit where he can best see them, adjust tones of voice or musical sounds so that they are within his range of hearing and so on. At present very little help of this kind is given to teachers who consequently lack the confidence to accept handicapped children happily much as they would like to help.

In some areas nursery schools and day nurseries have been established on the same site so that there is variety in provision for the under-fives depending on the needs and wishes of the parents. Most children who attend nursery school now do so on a part-time basis. Some nursery schools have extra accommodation specifically designed for providing facilities for parents and children who visit on a casual basis. Parents can accompany the child and stay while the child plays with other children and makes use of the facilities available. Provision is informal; parents are encouraged to make themselves a cup of tea and perhaps chat with other parents while their children play safely. The children are supervised by trained staff, some of whom may also work in the nursery at times. The provision is similar to that provided at 'drop-in' centres.

In the playgroup

The unique contribution of the playgroup movement is that it works on the belief that the child and his parents are a unit. Most educationists pay intellectual tribute to this idea but very little of our education system has so far been based on the reality. The playgroup movement began with parents and works through them. It is not so much a matter of *involving* parents as being the *responsibility* of parents and this is the main difference between playgroups and maintained schools. Maintained schools are beginning to welcome some involvement of parents, playgroups would not exist without them.

The good playgroup offers much of what the nursery school can give to children, but it may be necessary to discuss some of the differences between them which alter the role of adults. In some ways the leader of a playgroup has a more difficult job to do than the head teacher of a nursery school. She is trying to reproduce what she considers to be the best features of nursery education but at the same time working within the principles established by the playgroup movement. The premises used by the playgroup were probably not designed for use by children and the playgroup leader has to use ingenuity and effort to make them attractive, safe and suitable. She will find that the social services department is usually willing to give guidance about the regulations affecting playgroup premises and one of their representatives will make a visit of inspection before registering the playgroup. The regulations may be interpreted flexibly by the local authority if it is considered that there is urgent need for a playgroup in the area.

The playgroup leader has many obstacles to overcome. Often premises have little space for storage; she may have landlords who are not entirely sympathetic with what she is trying to do and do not understand what young children need; her helpers although willing and enthusiastic are usually not trained; she may feel that her own qualifications may not be completely adequate or up-to-date.

All this means that the playgroup leader is deeply concerned with background planning and contriving. She needs ability to organise and to lead as well as to cooperate with landlords, committee members, helpers and parents. She lacks much of the security which the head teacher of a maintained nursery school enjoys. She needs to be flexible and adaptable but must resist temptations to lower standards. She may find it takes a great deal of time to make and collect play material and then a good deal more to maintain and mend it. She has to make a constant effort to add to her own knowledge of what children need and the techniques of the organisation of groups. At the same time she has to inspire and help her assistants to observe children and learn about how they mature so that they get into the habit of looking at each child in the group to see how he is using his equipment of body and mind and how his character and personality are emerging and developing. There are many avenues of help for her and her assistants these days: television and radio programmes, books and articles about children and their needs, classes and courses held for playgroup helpers, and discussion groups arranged by interested organisations.

When she is face to face with the children she must put aside her problems, anxieties and frustrations and centre her activities on their needs. In the early days of a new playgroup when the children are strange to each other and to the adults they may need a good deal of help before they will be able to play freely but after some time things will become easier. The children will gain confidence and play with more and more vigour and enjoyment and then they will absorb new children into their community. When their mothers see how they gain in independence and social poise they, too, will gain confidence and be ready to support the playgroup and to try to understand more about their own children. They will be able to help their children more when they understand that social and intellectual development in the pre-school years is as important as physical growth and health and that it can be fostered by play with the right material at home as well as in the playgroup.

Because the children so much enjoy the stories and songs they hear in the playgroup their parents will be encouraged to sing with their children and to read to them. They will find that the children's librarian at their local library will be only too pleased to help them choose suitable books to read from and collections of stories to learn and tell. The playgroup will form a friendly meeting place for parents bringing and collecting children and they may develop their contacts into neighbourly visiting so that their children have yet more opportunity to play with each other. In these days a well run playgroup can inject into a neighbourhood a fresh interest in young children and their needs.

On the other hand, a poor or badly organised playgroup can do actual harm. If the children are bored or frustrated by poverty of material, by cramped space, by a tightly controlled routine or by limited possibilities of play, then their social development may suffer so that they become noisy and rough or, if the adults are too rigid and do not understand their need for orderly freedom to play and to make messes, they may become timid and uncertain instead of robust and independent.

Most playgroups begin because the parents of pre-school children in that area see the need for one and set about organising it. In some deprived or disadvantaged areas the stimulus may come first from a health visitor or a social worker or from a church group but mothers are drawn together from the beginning and mothers and children grow and play and learn together. Fathers reap the benefit because their wives are happier and this reflects on the father and on their older children. Often father is drawn in, too, to help by making and mending equipment.

Some mothers go only to watch at first, then they stay to help in small ways, then often to take a regular turn at helping. This leads to going to discussions and meetings for helpers to talk about play and organisation and how children develop, and eventually some of these mothers may be able to attend longer courses for playgroup helpers. Perhaps they feel confident enough to become committee members, helping to raise funds and take decisions about the future of the playgroup. In ways like these the playgroup movement encourages parents to extend their knowledge and experience as well as giving the children an opportunity to grow further.

Teachers in primary schools are beginning to recognise and respect the value of the experience which parents and children gain at playgroups. In many areas the primary school headteacher and the local playgroup leader have established a good working relationship.

Groups of local playgroup children may be taken to the primary school to join in the singing at assembly, to watch a simple play which the schoolchildren are performing, to walk around a classroom and look at the toys and games or just to pay a visit to look at and feed some of the school pets. Staff from the first school may visit the playgroup to tell a story, play the piano for singing or perhaps, with the parents' permission, observe a child who may be experiencing problems. This liaison is of great benefit to all concerned.

In the primary school

The modern primary school is an exciting and interesting place for everybody concerned with it. In a good school everybody is important and everybody knows he or she has a part to play. The headteacher, in consultation with staff and governors, guides the policy of the school. Most schools now have one or two parents on their governing bodies who take a keen interest in what goes on in the school. They have an important part to play as they can put forward parents' points of view at governors' meetings and can also act as school ambassadors in the community explaining to other parents why certain things happen within the school. No school policy can be made to work without the full cooperation of all concerned — teachers, parents, assistants, auxiliaries, cooks, secretaries, cleaners and caretakers. Most people think of deprived children as those who either have no parents or whose parents are too careless or too busy to look after them properly. But children can also be deprived if their school is a poor one. They may come from excellent homes but if their school provides no stimulus for them, if they are bored or unhappy in it or if the adults make them feel inadequate and ignorant then they are truly deprived because opportunities are lost for ever and living personalities may be stunted or distorted.

In the infant school years to the children all adults are important. Although young children are quick to discover where ultimate authority lies, they turn to all adults naturally for help and information. They are still dependent in a great many ways and they need reassurance. If an auxiliary helper or a caretaker gives them this when they need it she performs as important a task as their teacher. It is the attitude of this adult that matters, not the amount she understands about education. If the adult to whom a young child turns with his question or from whom he seeks comfort takes him seriously, is honest with him and is truly his friend, neither sentimental nor cold towards him, then the child is in good hands and is being nourished. The older primary school child respects the adult who knows what his job is and performs it well. He may ask for information but he does not turn to adults so often for reassurance.

We expect the class teacher to be well trained, to be observant and to be sensitive to the needs of the children in her care; she should have an understanding of the development of children so that she has some grasp of the stages through which her pupils have grown and can look forward with confidence to the future stages they will pass through — in fact to be able to see each child as a whole, past, present and future. It is not the province of this book to discuss the class teacher and her training, it is rather to look at the role the teacher's assistant can play in the life of the children at school. But unless the teacher's assistant understands what the teacher is trying to do and why she is doing it she will not be of much help to her. They cannot work as a team unless their aim is the same although their roles are different. It may be that when the helper herself went to school methods were different and she may find it confusing at first to work in a modern primary classroom. One hopes that no one will be employed as a classroom assistant without training and part of her training should be to learn about modern methods of teaching and organisation in the primary school by observation and discussion.

The teacher's job is to teach. She has the responsibility for providing a classroom environment which will encourage children to learn. The teacher provides the tools and the material for each child in her class to develop his own gifts and abilities. She must also create a happy working atmosphere within her classroom so that the child can develop a trusting relationship with his teacher and confidence in himself. The good teacher recognises the individuality and uniqueness of each child in her class and, by close observation, comes to understand the needs and strengths of each child. Children of the same age can vary widely in experience, interests, ability and the rate at which they learn. Part of the teacher's job is to help each child acquire skills which will enable him to share in the culture of the society in which he lives, so she must help him to learn to read, to write, to use figures and symbols and to express ideas in lucid and articulate speech. She must encourage his natural curiosity and his powers of close observation and questioning. She must help him to explore and use the store of information which these skills open up to him, encouraging him to make his own use of the material which he finds in the way which is best for himself, perhaps forging new tools of his own as he does so.

In the modern classroom the teacher allows each child to work at his own pace and at a level appropriate to his abilities. Within the classroom learning and teaching is not cut up into sharply defined areas — what we used to call 'subjects' — each with its own rigid allocation of time on the timetable. The teacher recognises that it is a waste of time and unreal to cut learning up into bits labelled geography or nature study or mathematics and she plans the children's work on a more integrated basis. She also recognises that children of differing abilities and experience require different lengths of time to gain mastery of a new skill or to develop new ideas and tries to make allowance for this. This involves a great deal of detailed planning, record-keeping and the careful organisation of the classroom workshop. The teacher and her assistant will be involved in steady, hard, practical work in the making of apparatus and the coordination of materials and resources.

The modern classroom with its busy workmanlike atmosphere is successful because of the mutual respect between teacher and child. Individual, group and class teaching take place within the framework of the integrated day. A classroom of thirty or forty young children could easily become chaotic without thorough organisation and preparation. Children who have purpose in their activities do not find time to be bored, there is always the next interesting step to take, appropriate materials to work with and a sympathetic and understanding adult to help. The child can look forward to following his own interests in his work, working with a small group of friends and, at times, doing things together with the whole class and the teacher — telling stories, singing, listening to music or poetry, going for a walk or an expedition, dancing, having a party.

To teach successfully in this way a teacher must first believe in what she is doing. No method, modern or otherwise, works well if the teacher using it does so against her will or judgement, because it is fashionable or because someone (her head teacher, or her college or her H.M.I.) expects her to use it. So the teacher must be honest. She must also enjoy working with children and be willing to use her imagination so that she can see situations with their eyes. She will have been trained to observe children and she will have learned about their development but she must constantly use this knowledge in dealing with her children who are not figures in a textbook but real people. She has to plan what experiences they are to have each day and to do this she must know them, as they are, as they have been and as they may grow to be. It is obvious that she must be flexible and adaptable and willing to keep abreast of new developments in her work as well as to improve her own particular skills. A shrewd college principal recently remarked: 'We demand an almost impossible combination of gifts in the primary school teacher today — intelligence, imagination, health, energy, imperturbability and gaiety. The strange thing is that we get it — if not when she begins then very soon afterwards. The challenge of the work seems to develop it.'

A classroom assistant can be the greatest help to a busy teacher if she understands all that lies behind the work of the classroom and is prepared to support the teacher and accept her as the leader. She can take over many of the immediate practical tasks of the day's work to set the teacher free for her own work. She can, for instance, keep the class material sorted and stored; she can make much of the simpler apparatus; she can mix paint, keep dressing-up clothes in good order, collect money, mend equipment. The teachers of infant classes will almost certainly need her help more intimately with the children and will suggest that she take part in singing and story-telling and help with games or guide individual children in the use of apparatus and tools. She can comfort a new child, settle quarrels, suggest solutions to personal problems of rivalry or misunderstandings, look after sick children and deal with minor accidents. She can take children out of the class for medical inspections or clinics, or take a group into the garden to carry out a project approved by the teacher. She can help with the changing of shoes or clothes for physical education, with coats and hats and boots in the cloakroom, with tying a hair ribbon or threading a shoe lace. She can talk with the children, listen, answer their questions, and oversee the clearing of spills or messes. She can supervise, for the sake of safety, certain activities such as cooking or sewing or outside play.

A classroom assistant may be shared by two or more teachers so that she must be flexible in her approach, learning to work with teachers with different personalities and teaching styles. She may do more practical work and have less contact with the children in the older primary classes than with those in the infant school range. She may have special talents or skills which can be used throughout the school, for instance she may play the piano well or be clever at the maintenance of mechanical apparatus such as projectors and tape recorders, she may have a flair for display or be a strong swimmer with life-saving qualifications.

But the most important contribution an assistant can make is in her attitude to the children. This attitude will be formed partly by her own personality and partly by the training she will have had in the development of children. If she knows what to expect from them and can allow for her own immaturities she will enjoy being with them and can approach each child with respect and affection.

She will be able to enter into the children's joy in new discoveries and help to build up their trust in a reliable world by being honest with them in any information she gives them and in the values she shows them. She will at the same time be able to tolerate difficult behaviour because she understands some of the strains there are for children in their personal life and their school life. Because she supports the teacher she reinforces her standards and the children accept this without question. When adults in the same situation work in harmony the children feel secure and are free to concentrate on their own work.

The teacher's assistant needs to be strong and patient but she must not confuse patience with inertia: real patience is constructive and creative. She must also be tactful and discreet. Teachers value cooperation with the parents of their children. They know they have a lot to learn from parents and they know that parents rely on them and that the children must benefit from the mutual trust and respect that can grow between their parents and teacher. The classroom assistant often cannot escape from a part in building up a good relationship between teacher and parents. It is not her responsibility to initiate the relationship but because she is another adult helping to care for their children parents will often talk to her. She may even be a neighbour of the family. Her discretion must be absolute and her loyalty to the teacher unshaken. On open days or at parent—teacher meetings she may be present to help with displays of work, with dramatic performances or with refreshments and she will naturally be friendly and welcoming, but she must resist all temptations to usurp the part of the teacher in any discussion of the children. An indiscreet remark may be misinterpreted and may spoil or delay the growth of a healthy understanding between teacher and parents. On the other hand she may often be able to enrich the relationship between parents and teacher, perhaps by a pleasant introduction or by remembering some detail about the child for the teacher to tell to the parents or by helping to overcome shyness on one side or the other.

Many first schools and primary schools are trying to involve parents more in their work. This is a complicated issue because not all teachers are convinced of the need to draw parents directly into the educational process. Some teachers fear that parents will trespass on the 'professionalism' of the teacher and will cause damage to the child by attempting to usurp the teacher's role. Other teachers think that forming close links between home and school and involving parents in their children's education will increase parents' confidence and competence in assisting their child's development. Some first schools who attach great importance to the value of close links between home and school have helped to organise home visiting programmes. Trained teacher-visitors regularly visit, by appointment, the homes of pre-school children and take with them toys, books and games which can be left in the home for a specified period. Parents are helped to see the educational opportunities presented in play with their child and, in discussion, can be made aware of aspects of the child's needs not previously considered. Parents and children are invited to attend play-sessions held in the school and are encouraged to make use of toy and book libraries based in the school. The teacher's assistant has an important role to play in this work, welcoming hesitant parents into school, assisting at play-sessions and servicing and maintaining the toy and book libraries.

Many first schools now encourage mothers (and fathers where they can) to come into the classroom to share their skills with the children from time to time — cooking or a craft or music or drama, for instance. When a mother can do this there are advantages for her own child apart from what she can give to all the children. He is proud of her skill and sharing the experience of the classroom with her puts them together on a new basis — she doesn't come in only to talk to the teacher, excluding him. Then, too, the children get to know each other's mothers better and are able to see them as real individuals. The sound commonsense of a mother is often useful in a classroom apart from her special contribution. But there are disadvantages, too. As he gets older, into his eighth year usually, a child may begin to resent his mother following him into his school world; sometimes a younger child can't bear to share his mother with his classmates and behaves badly.

And how does the teacher decide which mothers to invite? Outright rejection of an offer to help can seriously damage the relationship between teacher and parent. Are all parents equally welcome? What if too many expect to be asked? If over thirty mothers all want to come and help in one class no one of them will be able to have her turn often enough to build up continuity with the children. Will this disrupt the class? If not all are invited how jealous may others become? Will there be bad feeling?

The wise teacher, with the help of colleagues and her headteacher will need to find answers to these questions. Parents do not necessarily have to help in the classroom or even want to do so. Parents' skills can also be used in making and repairing equipment, covering books, checking stock, helping in the library. Much depends on the way that the school is run. Parents themselves can make suggestions about how to help.

As in the nursery school, problems arise with the question of visitors to the primary school (see p. 155). Too many visitors can make the children unsettled and disrupt the teacher's work. Visits must be carefully controlled without giving the impression that visitors are unwelcome.

One way in which parents and visitors might help now that we live in a multiracial society would be to explain to teachers and children about some of their social and religious customs. Children love to hear about festivals and celebrations and about the ways in which other families behave, to hear new stories and learn new songs and games. Teachers need to know what are the assumptions behind some of their pupils' conduct and even to know, for instance, when they may be fasting. One of my friends has in her class in a large city children of West Indians, Ugandan Asians, Pakistanis, Greeks, Mauritians, Cypriots, Malayan Chinese and Nigerians. She admits that she knows very little about the family customs and aspirations of these pupils and that misunderstandings sometimes happen.

Because we are thoughtless, some of us are jolted to realise that not all migrant workers in this country respect each other or are prepared to work together. One student from Sierra Leone in a nursery school told her teacher that she preferred not to work with the group of children which included two Nigerians. Our West Indian parents have little in common with Pakistanis and the Greeks show no interest in the Chinese. However, the school their children attend is a common factor and if we could ask them to help us by telling us about their ways of life perhaps barriers might break down.

What has been said about handicapped children in the nursery school applies to the primary school. Headteachers have the right to refuse to admit handicapped children to school if they think that the school has insufficient resources to meet the needs of the child. Usually the advice of the school medical officer and the educational psychologist is sought so that, in close consultation with the parents, a suitable school place can be found for the child. However, since the recommendations of the Warnock Committee were published local education authorities are looking for ways in which they can provide schools with extra staffing and resources so that the less severely handicapped children can be educated in a main stream school. The teacher who has the day-to-day care of the handicapped child will need extra help and support from within the school. She may even need some extra in-service training. The handicapped child may also be in need of counselling and careful but unobtrusive help so that he can cope with the demands of a normal classroom.

Recognising some danger signals

One aspect of the adult's role must be mentioned here. It is the valuable part the nursery nurse and the teacher's assistant can play in the early recognition of disturbance in a child's development.

I have said (p. 125) that one thing adults do is to prevent dangers for their children. I also said (p. 2) that it is important for us to know as much as we can about the stages of development through which children pass so that we may recognise danger signals and seek skilled help. The experts who are finding out more and more about the healthy development and behaviour of children tell us that it is in early childhood that evidence of serious disturbance may become clear and also that if this evidence is recognised early enough specialist treatment may relieve the condition and prevent illness or breakdown of personality in later life. All workers with young children should be aware of this and be alert to report to those in charge of nursery or school any signs of disturbance at once.

We are all aware that certain physical conditions can best be corrected or relieved if they are discovered early enough and sensible workers are ready to report evidence of, for instance, poor sight, or deafness, or flat feet and bad posture, or rickets. But it is just as important to report signs of emotional disturbance or maladjustment quickly, and some of these are not always as clear to a worker as signs of physical abnormality. We will know that all is not well with a child whose play is unusually boisterous, aggressive or destructive over a long period, and speech defects such as stammering are fairly obvious, but other signs may be more subtle.

We should watch carefully the child who is easily distracted and whose interest is erratic and never long sustained. Again, the child who finds it difficult to make a choice of play material or who plays idly without apparent direction of purpose may be a mentally ill child or one who has lacked the stimulus of personal encouragement and approval in his early months of life. The apathetic child or the child who seems indifferent to the people and activities around him may be a child whose mother said 'Don't touch' too often to him when he was beginning to reach out to the world; or he may have overwhelming anxieties and need help. The same thing may be said about the quiet, obedient child or the child who is excessively tidy, and it is especially easy to miss these signs of ill health because such children seem to be 'good'. It is easy to assume that the passive docile child has no problems without realising that the child is unable to express his hostility and has a negative attitude to school. Children such as these give no trouble and do not draw attention to themselves. In a busy playroom or classroom, especially if there is a shortage of staff, such behaviour can easily be missed. All young children like us to provide a regular routine but the child who is obsessive about orderliness and insists on every activity being perfomed in the same way every time may be ill. If he screams with rage or panic when we alter procedure or change the order and position of material he will draw our attention to his anxieties but he may fall into silent despair and we, busy and occupied, may not notice.

The teacher and her assistant also need to be aware of the children in the class who have special needs and who may experience learning difficulties if these needs are not met. The child may be immature, over-affectionate, exhibit over-aggressive behaviour alternating with periods of being very withdrawn; speech may be poor with limited vocabulary and the child may have limited attention span and poor physical control. Many children may show weakness in one or two of these areas but the adult should be alert to possible problems where there is a cluster of difficulties. Some schools have devised simple screening procedures based on close observation of the children to help the teacher identify those children who may be in need of extra help.

The teacher also should not forget the special needs of the very intelligent or gifted child and should ensure that he is provided with a range of activities which will give him the opportunity to use his skills and which he will find worthwhile and interesting.

We are not suggesting that it is the duty of the nursery nurse or the classroom assistant or the resident social worker to diagnose emotional or mental illness, but it is certainly part of her duty to report to her teacher or to her Head behaviour which makes her suspect that all is not well with the child. In a nursery or school or Community Home where the staff work together as a team there will be constant discussions about the children, and this makes it easier for each member of the team to become aware of disturbing signs in a child's development and to discuss them with her colleagues.

Further reading

Blackie, John, *Inside the Primary School*, H.M.S.O., 1967.

Blackstone, Tessa, *Education and Day Care for Young Children in Need: the American experience*, National Council of Social Studies, 1973.

Bryant, B., Harris, M. and Newton, D., *Children and Minders* (Oxford Pre-school Research Project), Grant McIntyre, 1980.

Craft, M., Raynor, J. and Cohen, L. (eds), *Linking Home and School*, Longman, 1972.

Crowe, Brenda, *The Playgroup Movement*, rev. edn, Allen & Unwin, 1975.

First Schools Survey, H.M.S.O., 1982.

Gardner, Dorothy E. M. and Cass, J. E., *The Role of the Teacher in the Infant and Nursery School*, Pergamon, 1965.

Jackson, B. and Jackson, S., *Childminders*, Routledge and Kegan Paul, 1973.

Jackson, P. and Holt, W., *Life in Classrooms*, Rinehart and Winston, 1968.

Lucas, J. and Henderson, A., *Pre-School Playgroups*, Allen & Unwin, 1981.

Manning, K. and Sharp, A., *Structuring Play in the Early Years at School*, Ward Lock Educ., 1977.

Preschool Playgroups Association, Various books and pamphlets, P.P.A. Publications (Alford House, Aveline St, London SE11 5DJ).

Primary Education in England, H.M.S.O., 1978.

Ridgeway, L. and Lawton, I., *Family Grouping in the Infants' School*, Ward Lock Educ., 1965.

Social Services Departments of local authorities, Pamphlets and circulars on child-minders and playgroups.

Taylor, Joy, *Organising and Integrating the Infant Day*, Allen & Unwin, 1972.

Tizard, B., Mortimore, J. and Burchell, B., *Involving Parents in Nursery & Infant Schools*, Grant McIntyre, 1981.

Tough, J., *Listening to Children Talking*, Ward Lock Educ., 1976.

Tough, J., *Talking and Learning*, Ward Lock Educ., 1977.

Tough, J., *The Development of Meaning*, Allen & Unwin, 1977.

Van der Eyken, Willem, *The Pre-School Years*, Penguin, 1967.

Webb, Lesley, *Modern Practice in the Infant School*, Oxford, Blackwell, 1969.

West, R. H., *Organization in the Classroom*, Oxford, Blackwell, 1967.

Wilkinson, A., *The Foundations of Language*, O.U.P., 1971.

Yardley, A., *The Organisation of the Infant School*, Evans Bros Ltd, 1976.

Yudkin, Simon, *0–5, a Report on the Care of Pre-School Children*, National Society of Children's Nurseries, 1967.

Summary of stages in the child's growth and development

His physical development

At birth

Weight approximately 3—3.5 kg (7—8 lb).

Length approximately 50 cm (20 in).

Lies in position in which placed but can turn head to side if placed on back or face downwards.

Makes vague, large movements of arms, sometimes opening his hands.

Can grip firmly.

Moves legs less often than arms.

Lies with knees bent and soles of feet facing inwards.

Sucks vigorously.

Sleeps for about 21 out of 24 hours. No waking period is very long.

Drowses when not asleep or being moved and fed.

One month

Can lift head occasionally when mother holds him to her shoulder.

Will follow a moving object (e.g. a handkerchief) with his eyes for a few seconds.

Looks vaguely into space when awake.

His feelings

Shows alarm when lowered too quickly, or held loosely, or at sudden loud noises, by stiffening, throwing out arms, spreading fingers, crying.

Appears to dislike too much handling and moving.

After some time may show excitement at being put to breast, and may make grunts of satisfaction when feed completed.

As before.

Can scream with rage if left unattended for long. This screaming begins to sound frightened after some time.

Swings from pleasure to unhappiness and vice versa rapidly.

His social behaviour

At birth

Prefers to be left undisturbed.

Seems most contented when in close contact with mother's body.

Cries loudly when uncomfortable but stops when held closely or rocked gently.

When introduced to breast may not suck at all at first, but usually sucks well by second or third day.

His needs

Warmth.

Quiet.

Cleanliness.

Screening from bright light.

Introduction to mother's breast.

Firm, gentle handling, head supported.

Shawl or blanket tucked closely round to give security.

Being talked to quietly when he is awake.

One month

Seems to sense presence of mother and looks at her when she is close to him.

His muscles make slight tightening movements in response to being lifted up.

Mother can detect different cries for pain, discomfort, hunger

As before.

Regular daily routine.

Feeding adjusted to his needs and those of his mother.

Being talked to.

His physical development

Movements of limbs still uncoordinated.
Still spends most of the day
sleeping or drowsing.

Three months

Waves arms about in a controlled
manner.
Kicks and pushes his feet against
end of pram.
Can roll from back to side and
hold head up steadily when
carried.
Watches his own hands and feels
his fingers; clasps his hands.
When lying on his stomach he
lifts his head and pushes
upwards with his arms.
Can hold a rattle or plastic ring
when his hand finds it but
does not usually look at it.
Sleeps about 16 hours a day.

Six months

Can sit with some support for
long periods and for short
periods without support.
Can grasp objects, using his
whole hand. Can hold an
object in each hand. Takes
every object to his mouth.
Arms now move purposefully
and energetically.
Can pull himself up if helped by

His feelings

Smiles and shows pleasure by
facial expression and by
wriggling of body.
Is still startled and distressed by
sudden loud noises.
Seems by frowning to be
anxious at some times.
Becomes excited at sounds of his
mother's footsteps, or at
familiar sounds of preparation
for feeding or bathing.
Wriggles body and pushes with
his legs.
Cries when uncomfortable,
hungry or lonely.
Makes various contented sounds
when lying quietly.
Still swings from pleasure to unhappiness and vice versa
rapidly but lies awake and
contented for fairly long
periods.

Shows eagerness and anger
vocally and by kicking, arm
and body movements and by
facial expression.
Squeals with pleasure, screams
with rage. Still swings from
one extreme to the other
quickly.
Sometimes shows anxiety towards complete strangers by

His social behaviour

and panic.
Will turn towards the breast.

Three months

Watches his mother's face while she feeds him.

Constantly watches movements of people near his cot or pram.

Notices voices and will stop crying when his mother speaks to him.

Gurgles and smiles when played with or spoken to by anybody friendly.

Moves his body when held to fit arms of person carrying him.

Six months

Eager and interested in everything going on around him.

Will hold up his arms to be lifted out of cot.

Turns in her direction when he hears mother's voice.

Laughs, gurgles, chuckles when played with by mother or familiar people.

Looks unhappy when mother

His needs

Opportunity to stretch and wriggle.

Rug on floor.

Cuddling and being talked to.

A little longer in the bath to play and splash.

Diet adjusted according to health visitor's advice.

Plenty of freedom to kick and roll about safely.

Frequent opportunities to sit up supported firmly.

Knee-riding, finger and toe songs each day.

Companionship of mother and family.

Time to splash and play in bath.

Simple playthings such as rattles,

His physical development

His feelings

adult grasp. Then feels his feet
and bounces up and down.

Kicks vigorously.

Rolls from back to stomach.

Hands and eyes now work
together.

Eyes focus and he gazes at
objects and reaches out for
them.

First tooth may appear.

Practises many different sounds,
vocalises continually.

frowning and withdrawal.

Generally friendly, eager,
curious.

Shows anger when a plaything is
taken away from him by
screaming or kicking but is
easily distracted by a new
object.

Nine months

Very active.

Can reach sitting position without help and sits without
support for considerable
periods.

Rolls and wriggles about.

Begins to crawl.

Uses both arms and legs vigorously and purposefully.

Can now pick up small objects
with first finger and thumb.

Handles everthing within reach,
passing objects from one hand
to the other and carrying
them to mouth.

Cannot yet deliberately drop an
object but lets go one as he
grasps another.

If held in standing position lifts
one foot and then the other in
a tramping manner.

Babbles and uses voice a great
deal.

Top lateral incisors may appear.

Sleeps about 14 hours a day.

Shows pleasure by eager movements of whole body, and
kicking of legs.

Will show annoyance and anger
actively by stiffening his
body, kicking legs and screaming. Will sometimes throw
himself backwards.

Shows some signs of being willing to wait for attention if he
sees familiar preparations
being made.

His social behaviour

speaks crossly. Smiles with delight when she smiles.

Although generally friendly, does not respond with immediate pleasure and welcome to strangers but watches them quietly.

His needs

ring to bite, wooden cubes, large beads or cotton reels threaded on a string.

Diet as advised by health visitor.

Nine months

Extremely responsive and alert.

Uses his voice deliberately to attract members of family and 'talk' to them.

Understands 'No'.

Waves 'Goodbye'.

Claps or waves hands to nursery songs.

Shows pleasure and interest on hearing familiar words and phrases.

Tries to copy sounds made to him by adults.

Offers object to friendly adults but cannot release it unless it is held firmly by adult.

Will play peep-bo with familiar adult.

Is not welcoming to strangers.

Often looks at mother before smiling at a new face.

Will actively resist some change of activity by stiffening, kicking and screaming.

Safe place to crawl and play in.

A variety of simple playthings such as cotton reels, small bricks, saucepans and lids, a ball, a rag doll.

Sensible clothes for crawling and rolling about.

Time to play in the bath.

Companionship of friendly adults.

Simple nursery songs, finger, toe and feature games.

Three meals a day with fruit juice on waking and milk at bedtime if advised.

Daily routine adjusted to greater activity.

His physical development

His feelings

Twelve months

Weight approximately 10 kg (22 lb).

Height 72 cm (28 in).

Can pull himself up using a chair.

Can stand alone but lets himself down by holding on to chair.

Walks round cot and playpen holding on to side, flexes knees and pulls upright.

Can walk around chair or sofa, stepping with feet wide apart, crablike.

Can walk a little if hand held by adult.

Crawls rapidly.

Can hold a cup to drink from.

Likes to have a spoon of his own to hold when being fed.

Pulls toys towards him by strings or ribbons.

Can now deliberately drop an object and throws things out of pram.

Can point to what he wants.

Can make a mark on paper with a pencil or crayon when shown.

Puts cotton reels and small bricks in and out of box or mug.

Uses eyes and hands more than mouth to feel and explore new objects.

Growing independence leads to rage when thwarted.

Shows anxiety when left alone for some time by shouting and whimpering.

Swing of emotions less violent than when younger.

Shows little fear and much curiosity.

On the whole friendly and confident.

Fifteen months

Restless and active.

Stands alone.

Can walk unsteadily, straight

Shows impatience with inhibition of any kind.

Emotionally more unstable than

His social behaviour

Twelve months

Watches all actions of adults intently and copies many of them exactly.

Will watch another child and copy one of his actions.

Understands and will obey a simple order, e.g. 'Give it to Mummy', 'Wave to Daddy'.

Knows his own name.

Babbles a great deal using his voice up and down the scale.

One or two words such as 'Dada' and 'Mum-mum', repeated often.

Enjoys copying adults' noises.

Cooperates in being dressed and undressed.

Often gives objects to friendly adults.

Likes mother or familiar adult to be within sight.

Is no longer so reluctant to greet strangers.

Entertains adults by repeating gestures or actions they have approved.

Fifteen months

Can say four or five words.

Uses a great deal of vivid gibberish.

His needs

Opportunities to stand, crawl and try to walk in safety.

More simple playthings.

Protection from accident in home — dangerous household articles should be put out of reach; fires, electric and gas appliances guarded.

Encouragement and companionship of parents.

Songs, rhymes and simple games (e.g. peep-bo, ride-a-cock-horse).

Music from record player or radio occasionally.

Suitable clothes.

Good mixed diet.

About 13 hours sleep a day (not all at the same time).

Opportunities safely to explore and investigate all his surroundings.

His physical development

ahead, but is not able to avoid objects in his path. Usually flops down, crawls round and stands up again. Walks with feet wide apart.

Can kneel.

Can go upstairs on hands and knees.

Can put one block on top of another. Drops blocks and cotton reels into carton and tips out again.

Looks at pictures in books and magazines.

Four first molars may erupt.

Does not take playthings to his mouth often but may do so with unfamiliar objects.

Eighteen months

Walks fairly well, with feet closer than before. Can avoid objects or walk around them.

Can trot a little; finds difficulty in stopping.

Can pull and push quite large playthings, and can carry things about from place to place.

Explores and investigates his environment ceaselessly during waking hours.

Can walk upstairs with some help or by holding on to banisters.

Crawls downstairs backwards.

His feelings

at one year old.

Swings from being dependent on adult to independent action, rejecting adult's overtures.

Shows jealousy of attention adults give to other children and pets or to other activities by leaving his play and pushing himself on to the adult, pulling at adult's arm, etc.

When angry throws his toys on to the floor.

Often shows obstinacy and resistance to suggestions by adults.

Cannot tolerate frustration, by adults or by the nature of whatever he is playing with, and may scream with fury.

Shows intense curiosity about everything, but attention span usually short.

Swings easily from dependence to independence; from eagerness to irritation; from friendly cooperation to resistance.

His social behaviour

Understands more words than he can say.

Can indicate to his mother when he wants something or when he is wet.

Cooperates skilfully when being dressed.

Dislikes restraint and resists strenuously.

Still needs adult close by although enjoys exploring freely.

Can point to various members of family and familiar friends in answer to 'Where's Daddy?', etc.

Tends to show off.

Will shout and gesture and call to strangers as well as friends.

Shows interest in other children; watches them, will pat, bite, hit them, may hand them toys.

Eighteen months

Uses about ten words.

Shows interest in words and practices them.

Tries to join in when adults sing to him.

Plays alone for longer periods, although he still likes to know adult is close by.

Has his own method of telling his mother he needs to use pot.

Does not cooperate so well as before with adults in dressing, feeding and going about.

Often says 'No' to requests.

Tries to be independent.

His needs

Opportunities to try to be independent (in eating and dressing particularly).

Encouragement and praise from parents.

Much patience with his ceaseless activities and messes.

Many simple playthings.

Introduction to toilet training in a matter-of-fact way.

As above.

A few larger playthings for pushing and pulling about.

A great deal of conversation, singing and voice plays.

Tactful cooperation about dressing, eating and changing his activity (e.g. going to bed, preparing for a bath, coming to meals).

Giving of new interest if it is necessary to remove an object he is investigating.

His physical development

Scribbles a good deal.
Is now definitely right or left handed.
Can turn pages of books and points to pictures.
Can feed himself, managing spoon and cup fairly skilfully.

Twenty-one months
Walks and trots more confidently and can stop without falling over.
Can squat down to pick up objects.
Can walk backwards.
Scribbles, making strokes and circles.
Has control of bowels unless tired or anxious.
Canine teeth may erupt.

Two years
Weight about 13 kg (26 lb).
Height about 82 cm (32 in).
Can run.
Can walk up and down stairs, holds on coming down, both feet on each step.
Can make a neat row of blocks on floor or build a tower of six or seven blocks.
Enjoys simple sand and water play — filling and tipping.
Feeds himself competently.
Control of bladder fairly well established during day unless tired, ill or anxious.

His feelings

Will wait briefly to be shown how to do something.
Less obstinate but enjoys independence.
More stable, equable and confident, but wilful at times.
Will show concern for mother if hurt (e.g. if bumped) but shows some aggression towards her at times.

Shows self-will.
May have tantrums, nightmares, irrational fears.
At the same time is loving and responsive.
Can respond to reasonable demand to wait a little for attention or satisfaction.
Tries to be independent.

His social behaviour

When tired, hurt, ill or frightened shows much dependence on mother or familiar adult.

Twenty-one months

Understands much of what is said to him.

Joins two words in simple phrases or sentence.

Repeats adults' sentences.

Asks for food.

Pulls adult's dress or hand to attract attention.

Enjoys sharing experiences with adult.

Shows interest in father as an individual.

Two years

Vocabulary increasing rapidly — may use as many as 200 words.

Shows great interest in collecting words and names of objects and people.

Asks 'What's that?'

Begins to use short sentences.

Joins in when adult sings or tells simple story.

Enjoys picture-books with adults and talks about pictures.

Can point to features and parts of body when asked.

Can ask for food or help in lavatory.

Copies adults' activities with some understanding of purpose.

His needs

As above.

More companionship with father.

Simple stories, finger-plays and songs.

Simple games with adults.

Silver sand, water, bricks, dolls, shawls, boxes, a cart, and other simple play material.

A few hats, shoes and bags to dress up.

Opportunities for independence in framework of a secure and loving routine.

Comfort when frightened, especially at night.

Reasonable demands for obedience.

Calm firmness when necessary.

Freedom to work with adults.

Help in how to do things.

His physical development

His feelings

Two-and-a-half years

Climbs over furniture easily.

Can use a climbing-frame.

Can kick a ball from standing position.

Sits on tricycle, moves it with feet on floor or may use pedals.

Pushes and pulls large boxes and toys about.

Can paint with large brush.

Can manage fairly well alone in lavatory but needs help in adjusting clothes.

Full set of milk teeth has erupted.

May sleep about 12 hours out of 24 but usually less.

Often passionate and uncooperative.

Swings between rebellion and dependence.

Wants to be independent.

Becomes calmer and more amenable towards third birthday.

Three years

Weighs about 15 kg (33 lb).

Height about 90 cm (35 in).

Runs, jumps, walks on tiptoe, climbs, swings.

Can throw a ball.

Rides a tricycle.

Can build well with blocks, using deliberate patterns.

Tries to make bridge with blocks.

Paints confidently and scribbles freely. Draws head and face but usually no body.

Begins to pound clay.

Can cut with scissors, carry a

Cooperative, loving, friendly, amenable, suggestible.

Adopts attitudes and moods of adults.

Towards end of this year shows some insecurity expressed as shyness, irritability, self-consciousness, nervousness.

His social behaviour	His needs
Demands attention a good deal.	
Will play beside another child but not with him.	
May show jealousy of other children even in pictures.	

Two-and-a-half years

Now refers to himself as 'I' and 'me'.	Patience and firmness.
Make-believe play with detailed copying of adults and some ritual repetition.	Answers to constant questions. Playthings as above. Some dress-up clothes.
Likes to have adults' approval.	Interest in and encouragement of his play.
Watches other children with interest. Will sometimes allow himself to be used in older children's make-believe play.	
No real play together with other children.	
Constant conversation with adults and many questions, mostly 'What?'.	

Three years

May have vocabulary of 900 words.	Companionship of other children.
Talks freely to himself and others.	Encouragement and companionship of adults with background of consistent standards of behaviour.
Wants approval of loved adults.	
Asks many questions: 'What?' 'Where?' 'Who?'	As much independence as possible with tactful and patient help from adults.
Plays happily with one or two other children.	Dress-up clothes; opportunities for painting, drawing, modelling, building.
Make-believe play continues.	
Projects his own experience on to his dolls and toys.	Freedom and opportunities for vigorous physical play in suitable environment.
	Sand and water play.

His physical development

mug full of milk without spilling, wash his hands, button his coat (but not smaller buttons), manage his clothes in lavatory.

Four years
Weight about 18 kg (39 lb).
Height about 100 cm (39 in).
Rides tricycle skilfully.
Walks quickly and confidently up and down stairs.
Climbs trees, ladders, nets, jungle-gym.
Hangs by knees.
Can kick a ball while running.
Throws well.
Can hop on one foot, gallop, skip and dance.
Paints and draws freely.
Models with clay.
Hammers and saws wood.
Builds elaborate structures with blocks, boxes, planks.

Five years
Weight about 19.5 kg (42 lb).
Height about 107 cm (42 in).
Is agile and energetic.
Can dress and undress himself.
Can run, skip, climb, dance, jump, swing, throw a ball, and catch it fairly well, build with big boxes, planks, barrels.
Rides a tricycle very fast and can use a scooter skilfully.
Draws people, houses, aeroplanes and vehicles recognisably.

His feelings

Confident and assured.
Shows purpose and persistence and some control over emotions.
Approaches problems reasonably if treated reasonably.
Has adopted standards of behaviour of parents or adults to whom he is closest.

Self-confident.
Boasts, shows-off, threatens but also shows friendliness and generosity.
Shows desire to excel and can be persistent and purposeful in learning a new skill.
Shows good degree of control of emotions and on the whole is stable.

His social behaviour	His needs
	Stories, picture books, songs, finger plays.

Four years

Talks fluently. May have vocabulary of 1500 words.

Asks many questions: 'When?' 'How?' 'Why?'.

Tells long stories, partly fantasy.

May swear and use bad language.

Plays with groups of children.

Groups tend to centre round an activity, then dissolve and reform.

Sometimes has one particular friend.

Elaborate, prolonged imaginative play.

Shows concern for hurt children.

Can take turns but is not consistent about this.

When hurt, overtired, ill or frightened turns to adult for comfort.

Opportunities and safe space for vigorous physical and imaginative play with other children.

Large play material for building, as well as sand, water, painting, drawing and modelling material, Lego and wooden construction sets.

More advanced books, stories, songs and musical games.

Careful and truthful answers to questions.

Approval of adults in a secure framework of consistent behaviour and standards.

To be treated as a reasonable person.

Five years

Vocabulary can be up to 3000 words.

Asks many questions.

Often content to play alone for long periods, mastering a skill, but also plays with other children, especially in building and imaginative play.

Prefers games of rivalry to team games.

Group games often need adults to arbitrate.

Calm, reasonable approach from adults who can control his rivalry, encourage his serious attitude to achievements and counter his showing-off with affectionate banter.

Play material as for four-year-olds.

Books, stories, songs, music.

Support of parents on beginning school.

Skilful introduction to school

His physical development

His feelings

Sleeps about 10 hours in 24.

Six years

Vigorous and adventurous.

Uses body actively.

Enjoys using large apparatus for climbing, swinging by arms, hanging by knees.

Can somersault, skip with rope, run and jump, use climbing ropes.

Begins to use a bat adequately.

Moves to music with understanding.

Throws and catches more skilfully.

Loss of milk teeth begins.

Permanent teeth begin to erupt.

More unstable than at five years.

Swings from love to hate and back again rapidly.

Tends to be self-centred, obsessive, irritable, aggressive, rebellious.

But can also be loving, friendly, enthusiastic, cooperative.

Intensely curious.

Finds frustration and failure difficult to accept.

Seven years

Active and energetic.

All physical pursuits becoming popular.

Can walk along narrow planks, balance on poles, use bats and balls well.

Dances with pleasure.

Enjoys physical education periods at school.

More stable than at six years.

Independent and may be solitary for short periods.

Self-critical.

May be moody and dissatisfied at times but gradually becomes more self-reliant and steadier in all emotional expression.

Fact usually distinguished from fantasy.

Lacks control of his own energy

His social behaviour

May be nervous of active older children in playground.

Basically dependent on adults — parents and teachers — and needs their approval.

Enjoys stories about strong and powerful people (e.g. Samson and Batman).

Six years

Talks freely and is still interested in new words.

Is usually beginning to read.

Begins to move away from dependence on adults but needs unobtrusive help, and demands praise.

Is often quarrelsome with other children but shows need of their cooperation in his play. May have a particular friend.

Tenacious of his own possessions.

Teacher's standards often accepted, rather than mother's.

Father's authority usually unquestioned.

Seven years

Reads a good deal, enjoys writing his own stories.

Watches television with comprehension and appreciation.

Depends less on adults except for specific help in work.

Make-believe play becoming dramatic play.

Can plan and carry out projects with other children but still needs some arbitration by respected adults.

His needs

life by teachers.

Accurate answers to questions.

Much patience from parents and teachers.

Firm control over daily routine within which he can be allowed much freedom to enquire, experiment and explore.

Environment at school and at home rich and stimulating.

Encouragement for his efforts and praise for his achievements.

Play material which requires skills — Meccano, Lego, train sets, dolls' dressmaking, knitting, cooking, puppet-making, drawing, painting, modelling.

Arrangements for adequate rest and sleep.

Same as for six-year-old.

Protection against overtiredness.

His physical development

His feelings

and will become overtired and irritable.

Eight to eleven years

Period of great agility and vitality.

All physical activities carried out with grace, economy and coordination.

Games requiring exactness such as hopscotch, conkers, marbles, fivestones, jacks, complicated ball and skipping games, roller-skating, juggling, rounders, are increasingly popular.

There is a good deal of group wrestling and skirmishing.

Hiking, swimming, running, climbing hills are enjoyed.

General health is good.

Appetite sound and food is enjoyed.

Energy tends to flag suddenly but a short rest and more food restores it easily.

Emotionally independent of adults to great extent.

Need for acceptance by peers.

Deep satisfaction in intellectual pursuits.

Joy and delight in physical prowess and skill.

Usually good control of strong emotions except in mob situations.

Anxiety aroused by ineffectual adult management of environment.

His social behaviour   **His needs**

Eight to eleven years

Membership of group of own age now important. Individual desires submerged for benefit of group. Weak adults and nonconforming children despised and ignored.

Mob violence may erupt if excited by irresponsible leaders.

Team games; camping; collecting popular.

Boys and girls mix fairly well except for more masculine boys and more feminine girls who tend to make their own separate groups.

Towards the end of this period sexes tend to separate.

Rebellion against authority shown by rejection of adults, tricking them, complaining, dodging unpopular jobs, verbal battles. Competent adults are, however, respected.

Towards the end of this period child is friendly, matter-of-fact and cooperative with adults.

Opportunity to learn accurately about real world.

Rich academic environment.

Books, music, creative materials.

Reliable, confident adults and reasonable, consistent standards set and demanded.

Independence and trust.

Undemonstrative, steady affection at home.

Matter-of-fact, straightforward information in reply to questions.

Opportunities for games and physical activities.

Some suggested play materials

1 to 6 months	rattle
	small blocks
	teething ring
	smooth wooden figures of people and animals
	floating bath toys
	mobiles
	pram beads
6 to 12 months	nesting cubes and beakers
	soft doll
	saucepans and lids
	wooden spoon
	floating bath toys
	drum
	cartons and tins
	cotton reels
	string of large beads
12 to 18 months	boxes, tins, cartons
	cotton reels
	saucepans and lids, wooden spoon
	several cuddly toys or animals
	wooden train (simplest pattern, fitting together easily)
	hammer pegs
	hassock
	pieces of material
	bath toys
	beads on string or abacus
	the furniture of the house and the staircase
18 months to 2 years	all as above and bigger boxes to push about
	hammer pegs
	drum to bang or tin tray and wooden spoon
	posting box
	screw toys

wooden rings fitting on an upright rod

small teddy bear and several rag dolls.
material to wrap them in

building blocks (wooden)

a large wooden engine or horse to ride on

a rocker

a steady cart or box on wheels to pull and
push

sand in a box or big basin with mugs and spoons

bath toys

balls

basin or baby bath with water and some
mugs, spoons, corks

a few hats, scarves, shoes, handbags to put
on and carry about

2 to 3 years

picture books

dolls, dolls' clothes, simple pram and bed
(box will do)

equipment for 'washing and ironing' dolls'
clothes

simple dress-up clothes

tea set, table, chairs

water and things to fill, tip, pour, float

sand and mugs, spoons, sieves, patty tins

powder paints, large brushes, paper, giant
crayons, pencils, paste, blunt-ended
scissors

dough

clay

simple puzzles

balls of all sizes

rocking horse

boxes (wooden and stout cardboard) and
cartons and tins

bricks and blocks

large nuts and bolts

large wooden car or engine to ride

box on wheels

several stout wooden toys (lorries, cars,
trains) on wheels

simple swing

slide

drum to bang and trumpet to blow

3 to 4 years

as above (2—3 years) and

carpenter's tools and box or bench (hammers, clamps, saws, nails)

scissors (rounded ends)

pages from catalogues and magazines to cut up

scrap paper

larger blocks, boxes and planks

car tyres

climbing-frame

planes, engines, fire engines (wooden)

tricycle

wheelbarrow, wheeled truck

wooden constructional sets with large pieces, simple Lego

more realistic dolls and equipment

jigsaws with about 10—15 pieces

picture-matching games

farm sets, Dinky toys

simple dress-up clothes

a house play corner (use a clothes horse as screen at home)

books (good variety) including story books without words

4 to 5 years

as above (3—4 years) and

more tools (screwdriver and screws, bradawl)

nurse, doctor, spaceman kits, as well as plenty of adaptable dress-up material

ropes for climbing

play shop

garden tools

more complicated jigsaws

sequence-picture games

counting-board games

big picture dominoes

scales for weighing

glove puppets

plenty of painting and drawing materials

clean junk with glue, string, plasticine, rubber bands, paper fasteners and paint

wagons and trucks

5 to 6 years

as above (4—5 years) and

more painting, drawing and modelling materials

constructional and building sets with smaller
pieces
plenty of dress-up material
writing material
table games, dominoes, card games, jigsaws
animal toys
scooter
skipping rope
tops
football
more tools and better bench
more building materials
house and shop play material
dolls' house, family and furniture
model cars, farms, zoo

6 to 7 years

as above (5—6 years) and
needles and thread
large wagons
spinning tops
balls of all kinds
stilts, roller skates
sophisticated doll and equipment
musical instruments
electronic word and number games

7 to 8 years

as above (6—7 years) and
bicycle
kites
books of all kinds
much creative material
computers

8 to 12 years

as above (7—8 years) and
equipment for collecting (e.g. stamps, shells,
matchboxes)
more advanced woodwork equipment
conjuring sets
train sets
model sets
gyroscope
toy theatre
dramatic properties
draughts, cards, table games, chess

embroidery and dressmaking tools
cooking equipment
science equipment
sports equipment
books of all kinds
good painting and modelling and sculpting
  materials
tapes and records, musical instruments
electronic games
computers

Additional reading

Axline, Virginia, *Dibs: in Search of Self*, Gollancz, 1966.

Blackstone, Tessa, *A Fair Start*, Allen Lane, 1971.

Bowlby, J., *Maternal Care and Mental Health*, Geneva, W.H.O.; London, H.M.S.O., 1951.

Bowlby, J., Abridged version of above: *Child Care and the Growth of Love*, Penguin Books, 1965.

Bowlby, J., *Attachment and Loss*, Vol. 1, Hogarth Press, 1969.

Bruner, J., Jolly, A. and Sylva, K. (eds), *Play: its role in development and evolution*, Penguin, 1976.

Bruner, J., *Under Five in Britain*, Grant McIntyre, 1980.

Central Advisory Council for Education (England), *Children and Their Primary Schools* (The Plowden Report), 2 vols: 1. *Report*; 2. *Research and Surveys*, H.M.S.O., 1967.

Deverson, Jane, *An Octopus in my Head*, Leslie Frewin, 1967.

Donaldson, Margaret, *A Study of Children's Thinking*, Tavistock, 1963.

Dinnage, R. and Pringle, M. L. Kellmer, *Foster Home Care — Facts and Fallacies*, Longman, 1967.

Dinnage, R. and Pringle, M. L. Kellmer, *Residential Child Care — Facts and Fallacies*, Longman, 1967.

Foss, B. M., ed., *Determinants of Infant Behaviour*, 3 vols., Methuen, 1961—65.

Gabriel, John, *Children Growing Up. the development of children's personalities*, University of London Press, 1964.

Hooper, D. and Roberts, I., *Disordered Lives*, Longman, 1967.

Ilg, F. L. and Ames, L. B., *Child Behaviour* (Gesell Institute of Child Development), Hamish Hamilton, 1967.

Illingworth, R. S., *The Development of the Infant and Young Child: normal and abnormal*, 3rd edn, Livingstone, 1966.

Isaacs, Nathan, *The Growth of Understanding in the Young Child*, Ward Lock Educ., 1964.

Isaacs, Nathan, *New Light on Children's Ideas of Number*, Ward Lock Educ., 1964.

Lewis, M. M., *Language, Thought and Personality in Infancy and Childhood*, Harrap, 1957.

Millar, S., *The Psychology of Play*, Pelican, 1968.

Nixon, Robert E., *The Art of Growing: a guide to psychological maturity*, Random House, 1962.

Noble, Eva, *Play and the Sick Child*, Faber, 1967.

Pickard, P. M., *The Activity of Children*, Longman, 1965.

Pickard, P. M., *Psychology of Developing Children*, Longman, 1970.

Poulton, G. A. and James, Terry, *Pre-school Learning in the Community*, Routledge, 1975.

Pringle, M. L. Kellmer, ed., *Deprivation and Education*, Longman, 1965.

Pringle, Mia Kellmer, *The Needs of Children*, Hutchinson, 1975.

Public Health Papers, *Deprivation of Maternal Care: a reassessment of its effects*, W.H.O.

Sheehy, Emma Dickson, *There's Music in Children*, rev. edn., Holt, 1952.

Tizard, Barbara, *Early Childhood Education*, Social Science Research Council/ Educational Research Board, 1974.

Tizard, J., Moss, P., Perry, J., *All our Children*, Temple Smith/New Society, 1976.

Webb, Lesley, *Purpose and Practice in Nursery Education*, Oxford, Blackwell, 1974.

Wynn, Margaret, *Fatherless Families*, Michael Joseph, 1964.

Index